684
FRI   Frid, Tage

        Tage Frid teaches
        woodworking; shaping,
        veneering, finishing

DATE DUE

FEB 23 '82			
MAR 4 '82			
NOV 6 '82			
NOV 10 '82			
FEB 21 84			
MAR 18 '84			

Tage Frid Teaches Woodworking
Shaping, Veneering, Finishing

Tage Frid Teaches Woodworking
Shaping, Veneering, Finishing

The Taunton Press

Cover illustration: When bending wood around a small form, it's sometimes impossible to get the right number of regular quick-action clamps on, so Frid uses hex clamps that he makes himself. How to do it is explained on p. 14.

First printing: October 1981
International Standard Book Number 0-918804-11-6
Library of Congress Catalog Card Number 78-65178
Printed in the United States of America

Fine Woodworking® is a trademark of The Taunton Press, Inc., registered in the U.S. Patent and Trademark Office.

The Taunton Press, Inc.
52 Church Hill Road
Box 355
Newtown, Connecticut 06470

Contents

Acknowledgments

Almost two years after my first book was published, I finally finished this one — a far cry from my original agreement with The Taunton Press to write three woodworking books in 1½ years. Even with practice, it still takes a lot of time to write a book, and a lot of patience from the people who worked with me. I am especially grateful to John Dunnigan for helping to edit the text, to Roger Birn for taking the photographs, and to my wife, Emma, for being the extra pair of hands throughout the work. And a special thanks, too, to Dr. Peder Estrup for translating the chemical stains in the finishing chapter from Danish to English.

Bending
Chapter 1

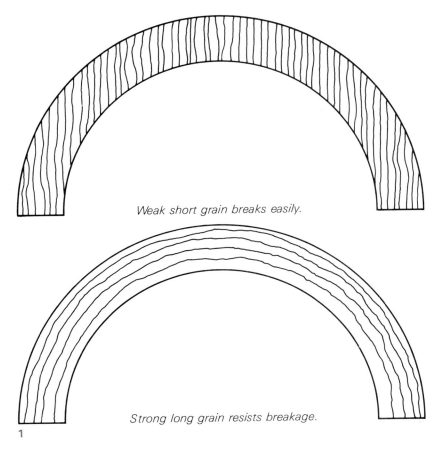

Weak short grain breaks easily.

Strong long grain resists breakage.

1

Steam-Bending

If you need a curved, solid piece of wood, the easiest way to get it is to bandsaw it out of a board. Bandsawing, however, means that the fibers of the wood will not follow the curve and the weak, short grain will break easily **(1)**. Another way to make a curve is bricklaying (p. 98). Sometimes it is even possible to find a piece of wood that has grown to the right shape. In Denmark, a boatbuilder or a woodworker could take a pattern to special lumberyards and order a naturally curved piece of wood to match.

Bending, either by steaming, laminating or kerf-bending, is another way to get a curved piece of wood. I never use kerf-bending because the saw kerf will eventually telegraph through the wood and the bend is not strong. It is just as easy to laminate, and laminated construction is considerably stronger.

Steam-bending is particularly useful in the mass production of furniture and in chair-making. Because it eliminates the need for some joinery and increases the strength of the wood, pieces can usually be made considerably lighter.

The most difficult part of the bending process is figuring out and making the forms — the bending itself is quite easy. In this chapter I will cover what I have found necessary to make basic bends in my own shop, without going into the complicated equipment necessary for bending large pieces of wood. It isn't hard to design and make the special forms necessary for bending more complicated pieces once you've mastered the fundamentals. If you do have to bend many large pieces, it's probably a good idea for you to look into factories that specialize in custom bending.

Recently, bending with ammonia has attracted attention, but in its current state of development, this is impractical and dangerous in the average small shop. □

Wood for Bending

Quartersawn wood, which is cut perpendicular to the annual rings **(1)**, is the best for bending. Quartersawn wood is difficult to find in small lumberyards and usually has to be specially ordered. Plainsawn lumber is not well suited for bending because it is cut tangentially to the annual rings, which makes it break easily if forced too much.

If the piece to be bent is not too wide, you can use a plainsawn board of the right thickness, because the section you rip off will be close to quartersawn **(2)**. Make sure to select a board with good straight grain.

Some larger lumberyards handle what is called veneer backing. This is the center stock that is left over from veneer logs, and it is close to quartersawn. These boards are beautiful and inexpensive. Remember that the centers of these boards contain the pith **(3)**; cut it out, or else the board will crack.

Some woods bend more easily than others. For example, white and red oak, birch and black walnut bend well, but mahogany does not. Of the common woods, beech and ash are best suited to bending. Most exotic woods will bend with work and luck, but the rate of breakage is usually quite high.

Generally, green wood bends much more easily than kiln-dried wood, which, for sharp bends, should be soaked in water for several hours before steaming. Industry uses green wood extensively, kiln-drying it after bending. Most woodworkers don't have the necessary equipment, so they have to air-dry their wood afterward. This takes a long, long time and most people can't wait, so they start by using kiln-dried wood.

If you do use green wood for bending and don't have a moisture meter, weigh the wood continually to determine when it is dry enough for furniture. Record the date and weight every week. When the wood has weighed the same for several weeks, it's dry enough to use.   ☐

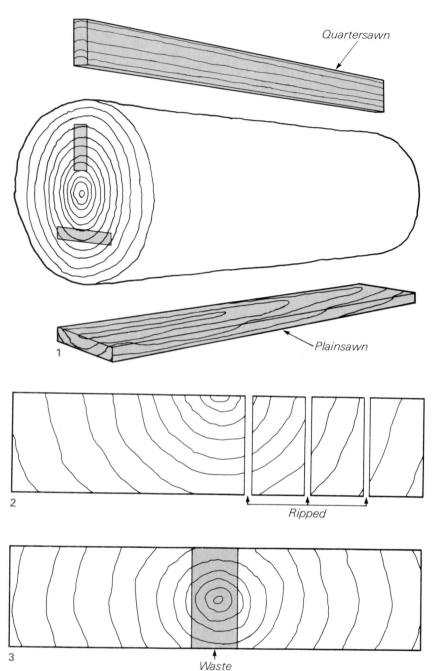

Quartersawn

Plainsawn

1

2   *Ripped*

3   *Waste*

The Steambox

Once you have your wood, you'll need a steambox and some device for making steam. There are elaborate and expensive steam generators available, but my setup of a 5-gal. can and a campstove works well enough **(1)**. Make sure the can is galvanized because the combination of tannic acid in the wood, moisture and iron will stain the wood black. Never use any iron or steel in a steambox. If you're going into steam-bending in a serious way, a better steamer would be a worthwhile investment.

I use exterior plywood, good one side, for my steambox (marine plywood is, of course, the best). The box measures 7 in. by 7 in. inside and is 6 ft. long — big enough for my work, with an interior cubic footage just right for the steam generated by my setup.

If you have to steam a longer piece, make a longer box, but try to cut down on the other inside dimensions. For example, if the piece of wood to be steamed is ¾ in. by 4 in. by 8 ft., the box should be 5 in. by 6 in. inside and 9 ft. long. Pieces to be steamed should always be at least ½ in. smaller than the inside dimension of the box. Never put in a piece of wood that fits too tightly, as the wood will expand and either break the steambox or wedge itself in so that you won't be able to get it out.

When you make your steambox, paint the good side of the plywood with two coats of porch or deck enamel and keep it on the inside of the box. Leave the outside unpainted, so that the plywood can shed any moisture caused by steam or water escaping through the paint on the inside. Assemble the box with tongue-and-groove joints, painting the joints with enamel and screwing the box together while the paint is still wet to seal the joints.

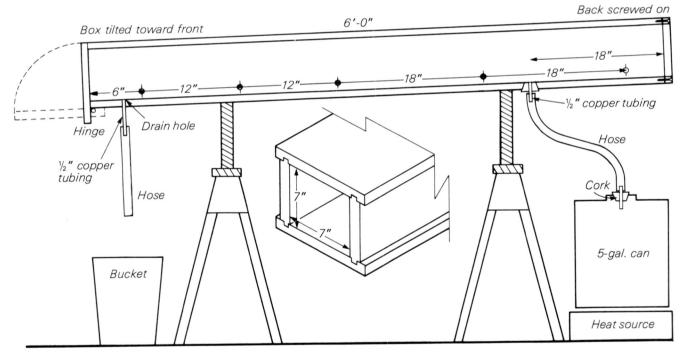

1

Paint one end piece and screw it on, but hinge the other end piece for a door and devise a lock to secure it. Make the door bigger than the box — the overhang makes a good handle to keep you from burning yourself while opening the box. Sometimes it's good to have doors on both ends so that if long pieces have to be steamed in the center, they can stick out the box ends. In this case, stuff rags into the openings to seal the ends.

The steam must flow around the wood in the box, so place ½-in. dowels between the box sides to raise the wood, elevating them about 1 in. to 1½ in. from the bottom.

2

Set the steambox on two sawhorses. The campstove and 5-gal. can should be accessible but not in the way.

When setting up, make sure to tilt the box slightly toward the end with the drain hole. The steam will fill the whole box, and as it condenses, the water will run slowly along the bottom of the box to the front. This will maintain a high moisture level, helping to soften the fibers of the wood.

I use ½-in. copper or aluminum tubing inserted into cork to connect the hose between the bottom of the box and the 5-gal. can **(2)**. Cork seals easily, but it will pop out if too much pressure builds up in the steamer — a good safety valve. Cement the copper tubing in with epoxy glue.

Keep the hose relatively straight so that as the steam condenses, the water won't get trapped **(3)**. With a hose as short as this there is very little heat loss.

Before you fill up the tank, consider that ¾ gal. of water will evaporate each hour with my system. Don't put in 4 gal. if you need only two hours of steaming. Although you should always test for yourself, the rule of thumb for most dry wood is an hour of steaming for each ¼ in. of thickness. Be careful not to overcook the wood, because too much steaming will weaken the fibers and cause them to break easily when bent.

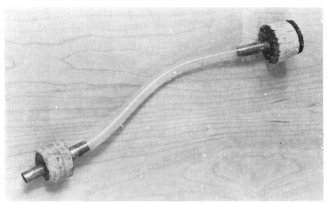

3

For a quick steambox that will work well, you can use a galvanized, aluminum or ceramic pipe.   ☐

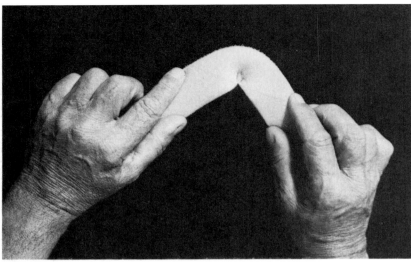

1

2

3

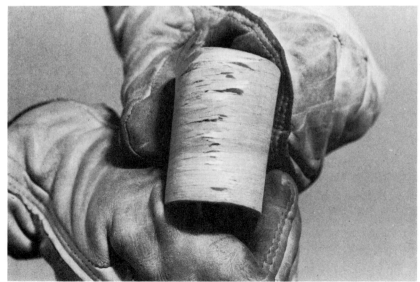

4

Bending Straps

When wood is bent, the fibers on the convex side of the curve will be stretched while those on the concave side will be compressed. You can see how this works by bending a piece of foam rubber **(1)**.

When a piece of wood is forced to bend too much, the outer fibers will start to run **(2)**. With more force, more fibers will run **(3)**, and eventually the piece will break **(4)**.

A spring-steel strap **(5)** with steel or angle-iron end blocks will prevent the fibers from running. The strap works by keeping the fibers from stretching; if the fibers can't stretch, they can't run. I prefer spring-steel straps because they will always return to their original shape and they give uniform pressure, but when using steel straps, keep wax paper between wood and steel to prevent black tannic-acid stains on the wood.

When you're using straps, the wood to be bent should fit snugly between the ends of the strap. Bolt the angle-iron end blocks to the straps securely. Have straps of three or four different lengths available. Then you'll have a good chance of finding one that is the length you need.

I seldom use bending straps unless it's a very complicated bend. I prefer to laminate because I usually make one-of-a-kind pieces, but even when making ten chairs I feel I have more control of the shape. Straps are most often used in mass production or for bending heavy pieces to be carved, where you don't want gluelines.

Before bending, it's a good idea to remove planer marks by sanding. An uneven surface is often what gets fibers running in the first place. Don't sand when you're going to laminate, because a sanded joint is not a good glue joint.   □

5

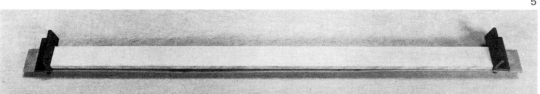

Forms

Steam-bending usually requires a form, and clamps to fasten the wood to it. Forms are often made out of plywood, but any inexpensive material will do.

A simple one-part form like this one **(1)** is made by gluing up several layers of material into a block thicker than the width of the pieces to be bent. Glue a full-scale drawing of the desired curve to the block with rubber cement and bandsaw out the curve, using the widest blade that will take the curve. The cut must be accurate, smooth and square. Fill in low spots on the form with auto-body putty and remove high spots with a rasp. Sometimes it is helpful to cut the form to a sharper curve to allow for springback. When possible, cut the bottom edge of the form to match the top curve, to ease clamping.

For sharper curves, it is often not practical to bandsaw out the bottom of a form because the form would be weakened. In such cases, drill holes in the form to receive the clamps you're going to use **(2)**.

If you screw and glue a block onto the back of the form **(3)**, you can securely hold it in a bench vise while bending.

This form, which I acquired from a former student, was bandsawn out of particleboard. Normally I would make this form from the cheapest plywood I could find, because particleboard breaks easily and dulls the bandsaw blade. Here, since the form is a solid block, particleboard is okay.   □

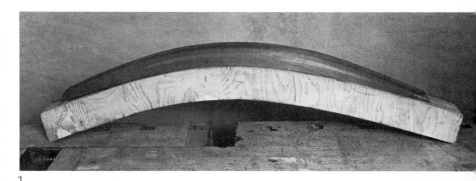

1

2

3

1

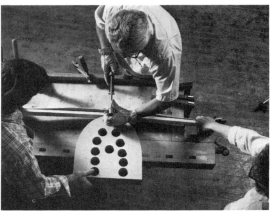

2

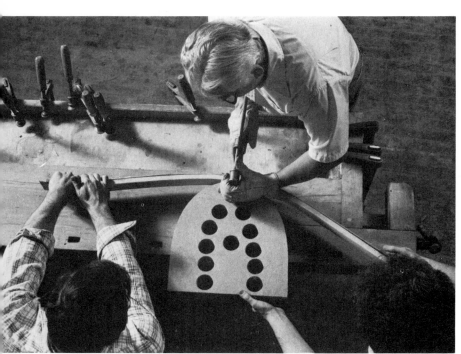

3

The Steam-Bending Process

When you have prepared the piece of wood you are going to use and have steamed it long enough to make it pliable, you are ready to bend. Using tongs and wearing gloves, remove the wood from the box and quickly place it on the strap **(1)**, which should have been warming on top of the box.

Both the piece to be bent and the form should have center marks on them, so that the wood can be lined up in the right place quickly. Clamp at the center marks first **(2)**, and bend both ends simultaneously **(3,4)**, clamping as you go **(5)**. Bend the wood to the form smoothly and carefully, but don't waste any time, as wood bends most easily when it is hot and moist. It's always helpful to try a test piece first, to check whether the wood is pliable and to get the feel of how it will bend.

The wood here **(6)** is kiln-dried ash ¾ in. thick by 2 in. wide. Steamed for three hours, it bent easily on this form. Drilled holes accept the ends of regular quick-action clamps. (More clamps are discussed on p. 14.)

After about 24 hours, I removed the clamps and the strap **(7)**. You can see that there is more springback on the left side than on the right. On purpose, I had clamped up the right side about a minute before the left to show that the faster you bend the wood, the less springback there will be.

Before taking the wood off the form, fit a retainer board with two end blocks to the piece so it will keep its shape while drying **(8)**. This will also help minimize springback.

Finally, remove the piece from the form and allow it to dry **(9)**. Drying time depends on the size of the wood and the amount of moisture in the air. The wood usually will dry in three to four days. ☐

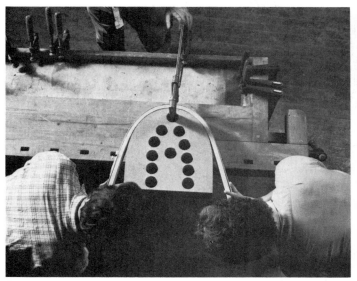

4

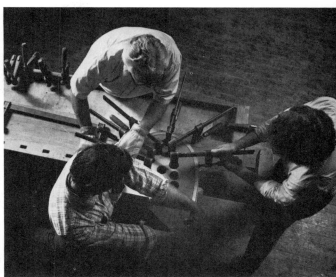

5

6

7

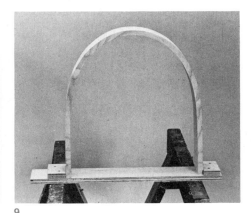

8

9

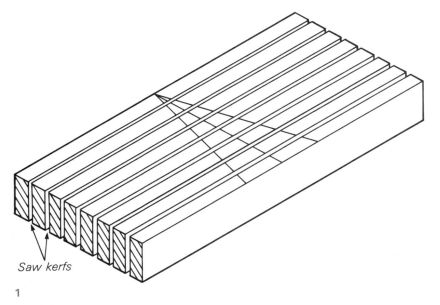

Saw kerfs

1

2

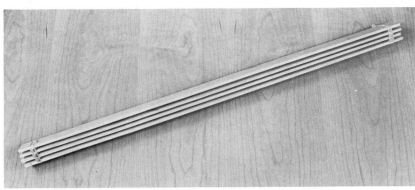

4

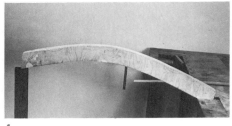

3

Laminating

When you are attempting a curve with a small radius, it is usually better to laminate several layers of wood than to steam-bend one thicker piece. Both steam-bending and laminating have advantages and disadvantages, and usually a combination of the two is most effective. In steam-bending, you only have to bend the piece once over a form, and there are no gluelines. A disadvantage is that it's difficult to predict springback. When laminating, you've got to contend with gluelines, but springback is minimal.

The thinner the laminates, the sharper the radius can be, and the less springback. Sometimes, however, in both steam-bending and lamination, when the radius of a bend is very small the curves may creep inward instead of springing back. This happens when the compressed fibers on the concave surface shrink and pull the ends in as they dry.

If you decide on laminating, cut the laminates from the same board and keep them in the order they come off the saw. After you run them over the jointer in preparation for gluing and put them back together, the grain will match and the finished piece will look as though it is made of solid wood. I use a triangular marking system **(1)** to keep the pieces in order.

For curves with a very sharp radius, you will often have to steam-bend the wood before laminating it. When steaming several pieces at a time, put small wood spacers between the laminates and tie them together with string so the steam can flow around each piece **(2)**. Take care to mark each piece and to keep the pieces in the same order during steam-bending, drying and gluing. Mark the center of the laminates.

Set up the wood on the dowel rack inside the box **(3)** and set up your form **(4)**, marking its centerline. When steaming is done, align the centerlines of the laminates and the form.

When you bend several pieces (or a very thin piece), using a steel strap is impractical. A ⁵⁄₁₆-in. thick piece of wood, plywood or hardboard **(5)** placed on the convex side of the bend will help prevent breakage.

Clamp at the center first **(6)** and work out toward the ends, adding a clamp at a time to each side **(7)** until you are done **(8)**. Here I am working with laminates that are tapered on both ends (p. 25), which are not the same as the laminates shown in the steambox.

Remove clamps 24 hours after bending and allow laminates to dry. Put scraps of wood between them so that air can circulate freely. Under average weather conditions with kiln-dried wood, drying will take about three days. To minimize springback, keep the pieces in tension with a string. This photo **(9)** gives the idea, but obviously these are not the laminates shown being clamped.   □

5

6

7

8

9

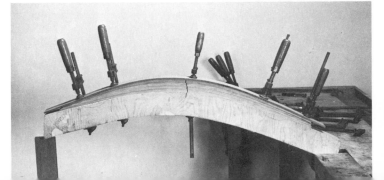

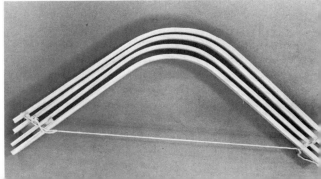

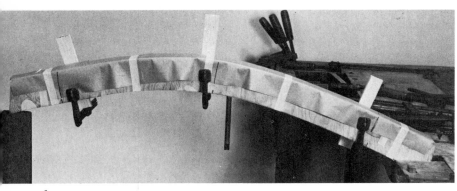

1

2

Gluing Up the Laminates

The kind of glue used for laminating depends on the job and individual preferences. If the wood is a light color (such as maple or ash), use Titebond, a light-colored glue. Titebond starts to set in five to ten minutes, so if you need more time, plan to glue up in sections or to get some help. If you are working with dark wood, use Cascamite, a slower-setting brown glue.

Have everything ready before spreading the glue. Cover the form with wax paper or a similar material so that the laminates will not be glued to it **(1)**. The three blocks of wood clamped to the form will serve as a backboard to keep the laminate sides flush.

Now, spread the glue evenly on both sides of the laminates **(2)**. This is essential for a good bond. Work quickly, and when all the laminates are covered with glue, put them on the form. Don't get nervous.

Begin to clamp at the middle first, and then put a clamp at each end **(3,4)**. Do not tighten down these end clamps all the way, as you want the laminates to be able to slide lengthwise against one another.

3

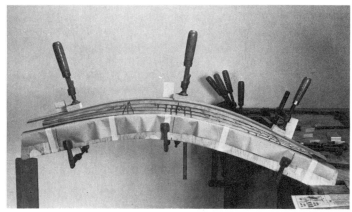

4

Before you continue to clamp, put a piece of wood as shown **(5)** to force the laminates flush against the three blocks already clamped to the form. Then continue to clamp, starting again at the center and working toward both ends of the form **(6)**. Tighten the clamps as you go. Clamp the two end clamps tightly, and you're finished **(7)**. Remove the backboard blocks as soon as the laminates are fastened to the form the way they should be, so that they don't interfere and get glued to the laminates.

Notice that on this form the bottom edge has been cut to the same curve as the top edge so that the clamps will be perpendicular to the laminates.   □

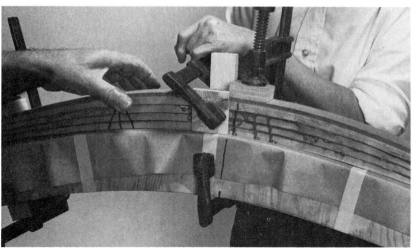
5

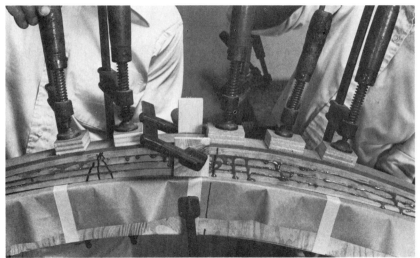
6

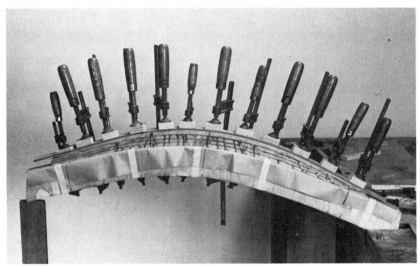
7

Clamps and Clamping

Whenever possible, I use regular, quick-action clamps **(1)** because they are fast and easy to use. Many times, however, these clamps can't do the job. Here are some different types of clamps.

The clamp that I find most useful for handling pieces up to 6 in. wide is made of ⅝-in. hexagonal, cold-rolled steel rod that is 7½ in. long **(2)**. Hexagonal stock is better than round because, for example, a ⅝-in. hexagonal rod won't move around when hammered into an 1¹/₁₆-in. hole. It will move enough, however, so that when you are tightening up the two threaded rods that go into it, the pull will stay straight.

To make this clamp **(3)**, drill four ⁵/₁₆-in. holes in the hex stock to hold the two threaded rods. Two nuts lock the threaded rods in place. Make a 1-in. thick piece of wood with matching holes to clamp down on the piece of wood to be bent.

Use a ⅜-in. reversible electric drill with an extension bar from a socket set to speed up clamping **(4)**. Grind one end of the bar to fit the drill chuck and use a deep socket to drive the nuts onto the rods.

You could use a wood dowel, with holes drilled for the threaded rods, in place of the hex rod **(5)**. The diameter of the dowel depends on the strength required and the pressure needed to bend the wood. Notice again the two nuts that lock the rod in place.

1

3

4

5

Before the form is set up and the rods are in position for clamping **(6)**, shellac or wax the form to prevent the laminated pieces from being glued to it, or put wax paper between the form and the laminates.

Place the pieces to be bent on the form so that the center marks of form and laminates line up. Tighten the center clamp first **(7)**, being careful when using the electric drill to get the same amount of pressure on both sides. Uneven pressure results in a joint that is tight on one side but open on the other **(8,9)**. It can also result in a flattened surface **(10)**.

6

7

8

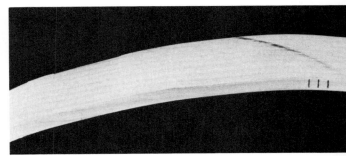

10

9

11

Here **(11)** the same pressure is applied to both sides of the clamp.

After tightening the first clamp, continue putting on the blocks and tightening them down **(12)**. Because it is sometimes difficult to push the piece down and get block, washer and nut on with only one pair of hands **(13)**, you might need someone to help you.

Here everything is clamped — twelve clamps were used **(14)**. It would have been impossible to get that many regular clamps on in such a small space.

12

13

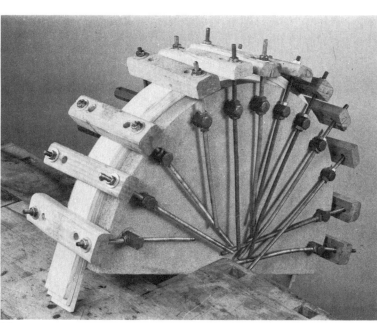

14

When clamping any laminates, especially when they are steamed first, don't clamp directly on the wood, whichever type of clamp you use. This photo **(15)** shows what happens if you do. The outside piece has flat spots where the blocks were clamped, the middle piece has a more even curve, and only the inside piece is perfect.

To get even pressure and to prevent flat spots, place a strip or two of scrap wood to clamp to on the outside. Plywood can be used, but for best results, especially with steamed laminates, use solid wood. If the laminate is ⅜ in. thick, for example, use two ³⁄₁₆-in. outside pieces. Don't steam these pieces and they'll give more even pressure.

I also use clamps made of Unistrut channel iron **(16,17)**, which, although more complicated than hexagonal clamps, are excellent for bending especially sharp corners.

On a corner, three of these clamps can be anchored to the same rod **(18)**, but they can also be used in the same way as hexagonal clamps. Unistrut clamps have a center screw that swivels, so they are able to exert very even pressure. The disadvantage in using these clamps is that it takes two people to operate them.

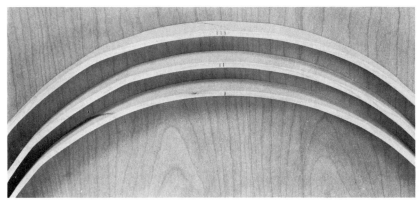

15

16

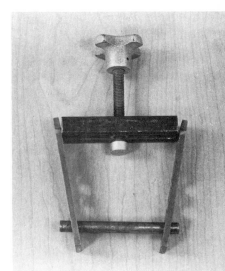

17

18

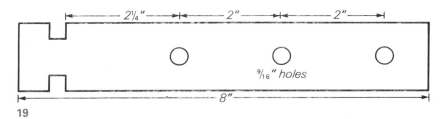

9/16" holes

19

Make the clamps out of Unistrut #P-3300, 7/8 in. thick by 1 5/8 in. wide by 6 3/4 in. long. A 1/2-in. Jergens flange nut (#19906) fits right into the Unistrut. For pressure, I use a Jergens clamp shoe assembly (#36307). Unistrut is available from the Unistrut Corp., Elizabeth at Clinton, Wayne, Mich. 48184; Jergens parts are available from distributors for Jergens, Inc., 19520 Nottingham Rd., Cleveland, Ohio 44110. I make the side pieces out of 1/4-in. thick by 1 3/8-in. wide cold-rolled steel, 8 in. long, with three 9/16-in. holes drilled in it **(19)**. The round piece that fits into the holes is made out of a 1/2-in. cold-rolled steel rod, 6 3/4 in. long.

In this photo **(20)**, regular clamps are used on the straight sides, but hexagonal or Unistrut clamps could be used there, too. This clamp is experimental and can certainly be improved, but it works.

In this case, the laminates had to be steamed first because of the sharp bend **(21)**. Notice the springback after the clamps were removed. After the laminates were glued together, however, there was very little springback **(22)**. I checked it a year later and the springback was the same. ☐

20

21

22

Complicated Bends

For complicated bends, a piece of steel or aluminum the same width as the laminates, and strips of inner tube make a good form and clamp **(1,2)**. Surgical tubing, which stretches more than the inner tubes manufactured today, is excellent to use. If steel is used for the form and the piece is going to be steamed, be sure to keep wax paper between steel and wood to prevent staining. Make sure the metal is thick enough so that it won't straighten out when you bend the wood on it. If you've ever wrapped a rubber band around your finger, you have an idea of the tremendous pressure an inner tube can exert. Also, the pressure is equally distributed over 360°.

Secure the form and pieces to be laminated, glued up, in a vise **(3)**. For sharper curves than shown, you may have to steam-bend and dry the laminates. Clamps temporarily hold the pieces in shape **(4)**. Don't put too much pressure on the clamps — as the piece is wrapped with inner tube, the laminates should be free to slide. This operation works best with two people. The inner tube here **(5)** was started at the bottom, but, depending on the shape of the form, it might be better to start at another point.

1

2

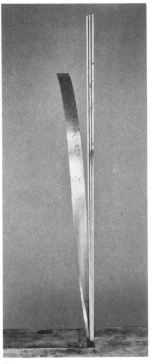

3

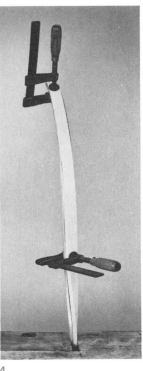

4

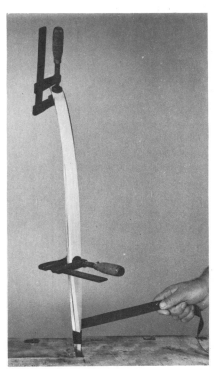

5

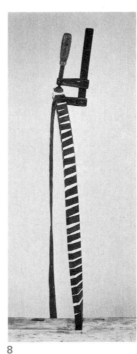

6

7

8

Wrap the inner tube around the form as tightly as possible **(6)**. Remove the clamp when you reach it, and continue. As you move up the form **(7)**, remember to loosen the clamps just enough so the wood can slide and you will get a tight glue joint.

Put a clamp on the end of the inner tube when you get there **(8)**. If you take the piece out of the vise, replace the pressure there with another clamp.

Here, the glue is dry and the piece has been removed from the form **(9)**. There was no springback at all.

The piece is sanded and finished **(10)**.

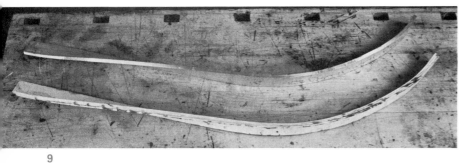

9

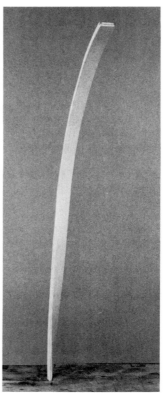

10

Two-part form Sometimes it is better to use a two-part form when laminating. It will allow more even pressure than a one-part form, but be careful in its construction.

You'll need an accurate full-scale drawing on which are marked all pieces with their exact thicknesses **(11)**. Notice that in this drawing radius A is shorter than radius B, so the two curves will be different.

When the drawing is complete, glue it on the form material with rubber cement, and then bandsaw it out carefully with the saw kerf on the waste side of the line. (For more about two-part forms, see p. 146.)

If the curves are each a part, but not more than half, of a circle, guide pins are not necessary to align the two halves of the form. The pressure will be even whether or not the two halves line up exactly **(12)**.

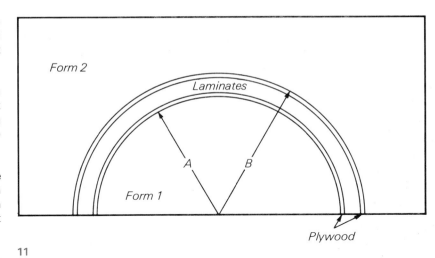

11

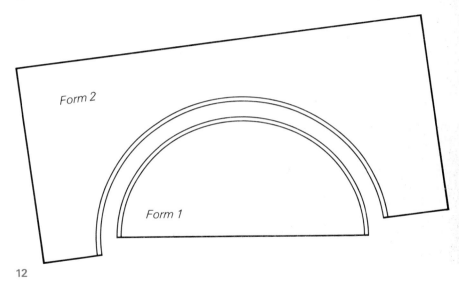

12

13

If the curves on the form are not part of a circle (**13**), you will need guide pins. To make them, dado out the ends on both halves of the form first, and then fit pieces of wood snugly in the grooves. Glue and screw the pins to one of the halves (**14**).

With the guide pins in place, the two halves should fit together perfectly (**15**) and give uniform pressure.

Now cover the laminates with glue, place them on the form and clamp up (**16**). Before you do, however, make sure to shellac or wax the form so the pieces won't stick to it, or use wax paper.

After gluing up, set the piece back on the form (**17**). As you can see, there is hardly any springback. □

14

15

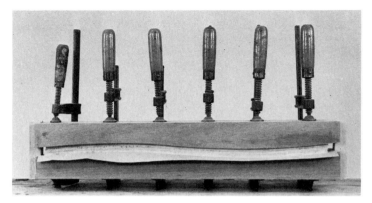

16　　　　　　　　　　　　　　**17**

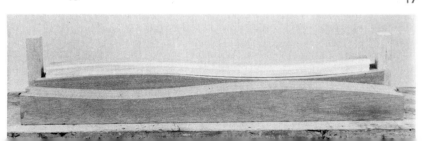

Compound Lamination

For certain types of work, you might want to bend a piece in two different directions. One way to do this, if the bends aren't too complicated, is to laminate the piece one way and then the other. When the glue is dry from the first bend, joint one edge of the piece and rip it into thinner pieces for laminating in the other direction. Use a sharp hollow-ground blade and you shouldn't have to joint the pieces again before the next gluing.

Here **(1)** four laminates are glued together and placed back on a form with a simple curve. The dried glue has been scraped off and one edge has been jointed.

The piece is then ripped into four new pieces for the second lamination **(2)**.

Here the pieces are put back on the form just to illustrate what is being done **(3)**.

1

2

3

The four pieces are then placed together and flipped 90° **(4)**. Now the four pieces are clamped back on the form for the second bend **(5)**. (When they were actually being glued, I used more clamps along with backing strips on which to clamp.) Finally the piece is glued together and sanded **(6)**.

In this case, the same form was used for both bends. For photographic clarity, I have eliminated glue, blocks and straps. Remember, when using a one-part form, always put the screw end of the clamp on top. The flexible head on the end of the screw will even out pressure.

This is the end of the piece after the second gluing **(7)**. Notice it is made up of small, square laminates. More complicated bends can be worked by milling small, square laminates to begin with. You can either bend freehand or use a form of wood or metal, clamped with inner tube strips **(8)**. □

4

5

7

6

8

Tapered Lamination

When you cut through a glue joint in a laminated piece, the glueline will show up **(1)**. It can be covered by veneering the piece, but that is inefficient.

If a laminated piece has to be tapered either toward one or both ends and you don't want the glueline to show, you can taper the laminates individually.

These two pieces **(2)** are tapered — one toward one end and the other toward both ends. Ash and walnut laminates are used here just to show the techniques clearly, but they could actually be used quite effectively as part of a design.

For making tapered laminates, you need a special jig to plane the pieces. In this drawing **(3)**, A and B show a jig for making laminates that taper in one direction; C shows a jig for making laminates that taper toward both ends. The jigs are best made out of solid wood. Here is one of the jigs bandsawn **(4)**. Each laminate is placed in the jig and sent through the thickness planer to achieve the desired shape. Here **(5)**, the piece that is tapered toward one end has passed through the thickness planer.

1

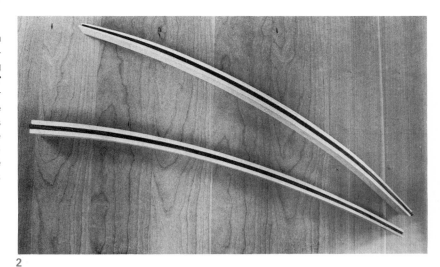

2

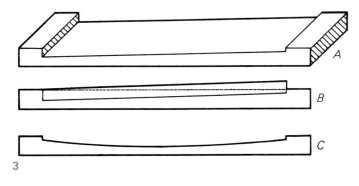

A

B

C

3

4

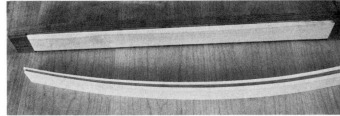

5

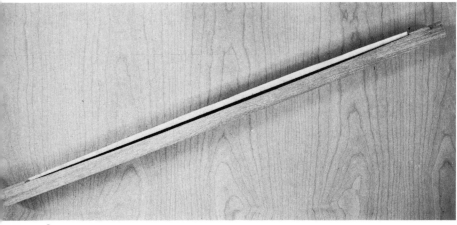

6

7

Here is a jig for laminates that taper toward both ends **(6)**. Notice that the laminate side toward the jig is jointed flat. The other side is sawed to the approximate shape to speed up the operation.

A piece with a clamp on it in the jig demonstrates what happens when the jig is passed through the thickness planer **(7)**. As the jig and laminates go through the planer, the pressure bar and rollers that push the piece through will force the laminate down into the jig, and the piece will be planed to the appropriate shape.

Gluing procedures and clamping techniques for tapered laminates are the same as those used for other types of lamination.   ☐

Scrapers
Chapter 2

1

2

3

The Scraper Blade

Scrapers are available as a simple, rectangular piece of steel, called a scraper blade, and as a blade mounted in a handle resembling a large spokeshave, called a cabinet scraper. Scraper blades are also available in a curved shape of varying radii **(1)**. These are called gooseneck scrapers (also swan-neck scrapers) and are excellent for smoothing out curved surfaces like the insides of bowls or moldings. Because of the irregular shape, there is usually some place on this type of scraper that will fit the work. Gooseneck scraper blades are sharpened the same way as straight scraper blades.

The scraper blade is an important, versatile tool for cabinetmakers and wood sculptors. It can be used for crude and fine work — to scrape glue, to smooth out a surface before sanding and to produce a high-gloss finish with lacquer or shellac. It's better to use than sandpaper between coats of finish. When an old scraper blade gets too narrow to use, it can become a tool for making half-blind or hidden dovetails. I feel that the name scraper blade is incorrect because, when used properly, a scraper blade cuts the fibers of the wood instead of scraping or pulling them.

The surface of an inexpensive scraper blade is very rough and does not make a clean burr when sharpened **(2)**. I use a Sandvik #475 scraper blade **(3)**, which costs about twice as much as a cheap one but is worth every penny. The polished edges and high-quality steel of a Sandvik scraper blade produce a much cleaner burr that keeps cutting long after others are dull. Because most people buy only one or two blades in a lifetime, it is a good investment to buy the best. I like to keep two blades ready — one for all-purpose work and one just for scraping lacquer and shellac.

The working edge of all scrapers is a burr, which, when magnified, resembles a small hook running the length of the edge. It's not hard to sharpen and maintain a scraper, but it takes a lot of practice to get right. Many people get frustrated and give up, which is one of the reasons you don't see scrapers used more often. Once you learn to sharpen and maintain the proper edge on a scraper blade and a cabinet scraper, however, you'll wonder how you ever did without them.

In sharpening a scraper blade, first file the long edges square with a fine, flat mill file. Clamp the blade in a vise and curl your fingers around the file for control **(4)**.

Hold the file square to the edge and draw it along in long, even strokes **(5)**. Let the file cut only when you push it forward; if you try to cut on the pull stroke, the file will chatter and mar the edge of the blade.

As you can see, the file leaves shallow marks on the edge **(6)**. It isn't necessary to remove these marks for rough work, but it is for fine work, such as scraping finishes. To remove the file marks, use a medium-grit wet/dry carborundum stone without oil. To prevent making a groove in the stone, which would round the blade edges, work on different areas of the stone **(7,8)**, not in any one spot. Using the edge of the stone **(9)** will help prevent ruining the face.

4

5

6

7

8

9

10

11

12

Now you can remove the few remaining fine scratches with a Belgian clay waterstone and water **(10)**. I don't like to use oil because it mixes with particles from the stone and gets on my hands and the bench. Before I know it, the work gets oily, too. The edge a waterstone produces is just as good as an oilstone's, and it cuts the metal faster. Don't rock the stone — the blade edge must remain flat and square. Again, make sure to work on different areas of the stone so grooves don't form in it.

When honing, give the edge about ten strokes, and then hone the sides of the blade ten strokes each. Repeat the process, this time with nine strokes, and continue until you get down to one stroke on each side. Use your finger to steady the blade when honing the sides, as I do here **(11,12)**.

Now you are ready to give the blade its cutting edge. This is done by stroking with a burnisher, which is a piece of steel, harder than the blade, that puts on the cutting burr. Burnishers come in different sizes and shapes — triangular, round and oval — but I think the back of a chisel works just as well as anything and then I don't have to buy another tool.

If you buy a good scraper blade to begin with, such as the Sandvik, you won't have to go through the filing and honing steps the first time. The blade will be ready for the burr as soon as you bring it home.

Before putting on the burr, place a few drops of machine oil on the scraper blade and the back of the chisel **(13)**. The oil prevents the chatter of steel on steel, which will nick the burr once it's made.

Hold the chisel at an angle of about 85° to the face of the scraper **(14)** and draw it toward you in a smooth stroke that is the full length of the blade **(15,16,17)**. Pulling the chisel lets you keep the pressure, which should be very light, consistent — never push. Tilt the chisel so that you only use the back edge. In this photograph **(16)**, the angle is exaggerated to show how to hold the chisel. If the chisel is 1 in. wide, the gap in front should be about 1/32 in.

13

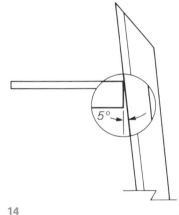

14

15

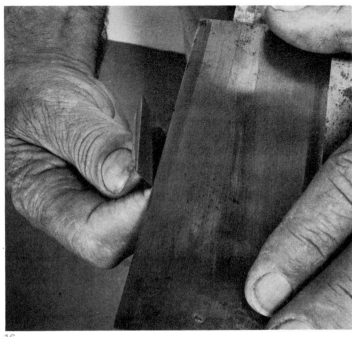

16

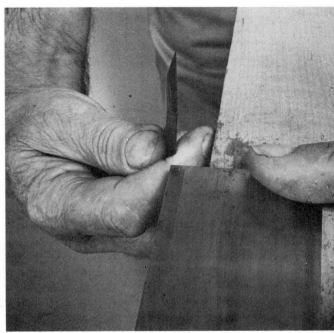

17

After two or three light passes you should have a small, even burr. Move your finger across the face of the scraper after each stroke to feel how big the burr is **(18)**. When you're finished, you should barely be able to feel it. Don't cut yourself.

Most people usually get too excited and burnish too hard the first time they sharpen a scraper blade. The result is a big hook that digs too far into the wood. This is okay for rough work, like scraping glue, but for fine finishing you need a light touch when burnishing the cutting edge.

When the burr feels right, put one on each of the remaining three edges. Then try the blade to see if it cuts; if it doesn't, go over it once or twice more until it does.

When a scraper blade gets dull, there's no need to refile and hone each time. Simply recondition the burr. First put a little oil on both faces of the scraper and on the back of the chisel **(19)**. Then smooth the oil with your finger — which finger to use is up to you. Burnish the old burr down, and then pull it back up again.

Lay the blade flat on the edge of the bench. Be sure the chisel is flat **(20)**, not as it is here **(21)**, because the cutting edge would be ruined if you did it this way. Let your index finger slide along the edge of the bench so you don't cut into your other hand. With your thumb holding the chisel flat against the surface of the blade and the chisel tilted slightly in the direction in which it is moving, go the full length of the blade with every stroke. Use light pressure in the beginning. As you go along, you can get more and more excited and put more and more pressure on until the burr is flattened.

The chisel can be moved back and forth in this case, but be sure to go the full length of the blade each time and to tilt the chisel slightly. Now you're ready to raise the burr, as before. You can do this five or six times before having to refile and hone.

For rough work and even for use before sanding, I simply file the edge, without stoning. I leave on the burr produced by the file, burnish it flat and raise it back up again. An edge treated this way will cut as well as if it were stoned, but it will have microscopic nicks. Since sandpaper will remove any nicks in the work, this is okay.

With the scraper blade sharpened, it's ready to be used. If it is sharpened correctly, it will make fine shavings, not dust.

18

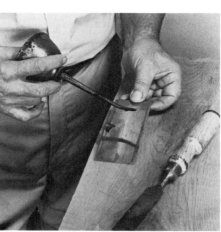

19

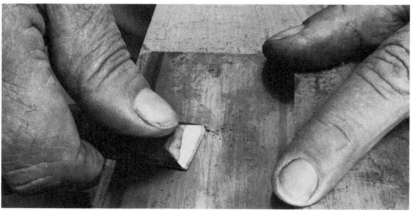

20

21

You can either push or pull a scraper blade, but pulling is better because you have more control. For rough work, such as removing glue, paper or old finish, it's okay to push.

When pushing, curl your fingers around the ends of the blade and press your thumbs in the center to bow the blade slightly **(22)**. When pulling the blade toward you, your four fingers of each hand will support the back of the blade and keep it straight. Your two thumbs will be in the front, controlling the angle of the blade **(23)**.

When this blade was pushed, it cut only in the center, so the shaving produced was not very wide **(24)**. When the same blade was pulled, the cut was as wide as the blade **(25)**.

22

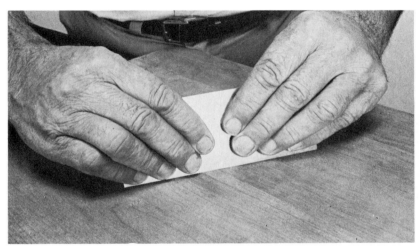

23

24

25

26

27

Don't hold the blade at too shallow an angle **(26)**, as it will scrape instead of cut and dull quickly. Held at the correct angle, about 80° **(27)**, the blade will last for a long time. It will also cut better and more evenly if held askew to the grain direction but moved parallel to the grain **(28)**. Reverse the angle of the blade to your body after each stroke **(29,30)**. If the blade were to dig down a little, making a slight groove, and you worked the blade the same way every time, the groove would get bigger and bigger. Think of a road with a small hole; every time a car passes over it, the size of the hole increases slightly, until finally there is a large pothole.

After reading this and trying to sharpen a scraper several times, you might be the most frustrated person in the world. But don't give up. All of a sudden it will work out right, if you don't get too excited. Remember the light touch. □

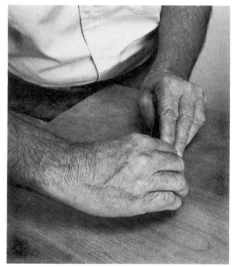

29

28

30

The Cabinet Scraper

A cabinet scraper has many uses. It can remove old finishes, dried glue and paper that is stuck to veneer. Its main function, if sharpened correctly and used right, is to put a fine surface on burled or figured wood or delicate veneer before sanding.

A cabinet scraper has two screws to hold its blade in place **(1)**, and a set screw **(2)** to flex the blade. The blade of a cabinet scraper is sharpened like a scraper blade, except it has a bevel. Also, its burr should be slightly larger.

To begin, clamp the cabinet-scraper blade to the bench with its bevel up and overhanging the bench edge. With a flat mill file held in both hands, file the bevel at an angle of 25° to 30° **(3)**. This angle makes the bevel about twice as long as the blade is thick — a quick way to judge if an angle is correct.

File until there is a burr on the back, being careful not to file the blade to a convex shape. It is better, in fact, to file it a hair concave. When the set screw is tightened, the blade will straighten out and take a shaving the full width of the blade. As you file, knock the corners off the blade so they won't dig into the work later.

Make a handle for holding the blade when sharpening **(4)**. A piece of scrap wood with a saw kerf in it for the blade works well and will prevent you from cutting yourself too often. Some people sharpen both edges of the blade, but I don't. When you're trying to work with this tool, it is too dangerous to have a sharp edge sticking up.

1

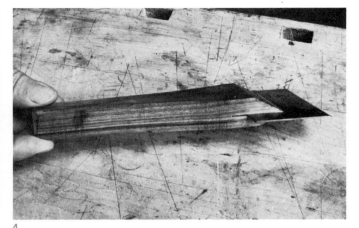

2

3   4

5

Remove the file marks from the bevel with a medium-grit sharpening stone **(5)**. I use a wet/dry carborundum stone without oil. Don't turn over the blade to remove the burr because the stone will leave scratches there.

Next, hone the edge on a fine-grit stone. I use a Belgian clay waterstone. Move the bevel back and forth over the stone ten times, then flip the blade and do the other side about ten times **(6,7)**. Do each side nine times, then eight, and so on, until you get down to one time each. The burr should be gone. (In these pictures it looks like I'm losing fingers but don't worry, they're just tucked out of the way.)

6

7

After the edge is honed, put the cutting burr on with a burnisher. The size cutting burr you put on depends on the kind of work the cabinet scraper is going to do. You'll want a larger burr to remove old finishes or glue than you will for finer work. Experience helps here. Try to start out with a small burr and if that doesn't work, put on one that's a little bigger until it works right.

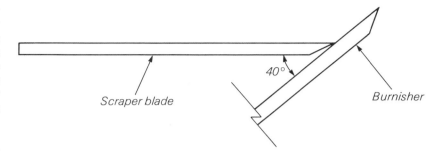

8

The first step in putting on the burr is to apply a little machine oil to the blade so the burnisher will slide smoothly. Hold the burnisher at an angle of about 40° to the face of the blade **(8)** and draw it toward you until an even burr forms **(9,10)**. When using a chisel for a burnisher, tilt it slightly so that you work with only one edge. Always use a light touch. It is much better to go over the edge two or three times rather than to try to put on the burr with just one stroke.

9

After each stroke, feel how big the burr is with your finger, but be careful that you don't cut yourself.

Now set the cabinet scraper blade into its handle, making sure that the set screw is out of the way. Put one or two pieces of paper under the front of the scraper sole, depending on how much of a shaving you want to remove, and slip in the blade so it rests on the bench. Push down the blade with your index fingers and use your two middle fingers to tighten the screws that hold the blade **(11)**. Tighten the screws with a screwdriver before using the scraper.

10

11

When the blade is secured, tighten the set screw **(12)** so it just touches the blade, which will help prevent chattering. Then make a test cut. If only the two corners of the blade are cutting, tighten the screw a little more until the whole blade cuts a shaving.

Here the blade is set correctly and you can see that the shaving is as wide as the blade **(13)**. With the cabinet scraper set like this, you'll remove a shaving about the thickness of the paper you put under the front of the sole in the beginning.

The cabinet scraper was designed for pushing; the handles were designed to fit the palms of your hands. Many people use this tool by pulling it, but then it chatters and won't cut.

When using a cabinet scraper, use the weight of your body to hold it down and keep it from chattering **(14)**. If the scraper still chatters, the blade is probably set too deep, so take it out and reset it using fewer or thinner papers under the front of the sole.

When the blade dulls, you needn't go through the whole process of refiling and honing. Just recondition the burr. Place the blade on a bench, burr side up, and put a little oil on it and the burnisher. Flatten out the burr with one edge of the burnisher, using a light hand at first, and adding more pressure with each pass **(15)**. About five passes should do it. Make sure to keep the edge of the burnisher flat on the surface, and slide one finger along the edge of the bench to keep from cutting yourself.

When the burr is flattened, pull it back up the same way as before. You can recondition the burr like this five or six times, depending on the job, before you will have to refile and hone the blade. □

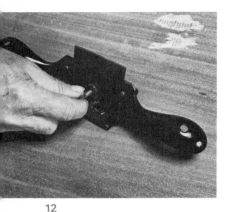

12

13

15

14

Carving
Chapter 3

Types of Carving

The term woodcarving encompasses a wide range of specialties including figure, letter and relief carving. Generally, figure carving entails working in the round as when making a bowl or a statue. Relief carving is the process of making shapes stand out from their background, such as carving a shell on the front of a highboy. Letter carving is one of the most difficult types of carving to learn. After you've finally selected the right style of letter to express the message, you've got to do the work without making any mistakes. If the gouge slips when finishing the very last letter, you've got to start all over again.

The best woodcarvers usually possess a good feeling for form and shape along with a sound knowledge of wood as a material. Both are necessary to take full advantage of the natural beauty of the wood. In this chapter, I will show how to carve a simple bowl to illustrate basic techniques, and I will also demonstrate how to use common carving tools. ☐

Tools

If you want to learn how to carve, the first thing to do is to buy some good woodcarving tools. Make sure that they fit comfortably in your hand and that they take and hold a good edge. Carving tools are available in a variety of shapes and sizes, for light or heavy work. Some are especially made for letter or relief carving. It's a good idea to start out with a small set and then add the type of tools for the kind of work you want to do.

Gouges are the most important tools for carving **(1)**. For the type of carving I do, I prefer medium-size tools (about 5 in. to 6 in. long). These are easy to handle, but they can be hit with a mallet.

The drawing **(2)** shows the types of tools I have found necessary for carving. I also use regular flat chisels, for outside carving.

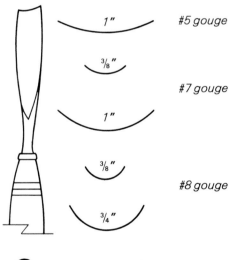

1

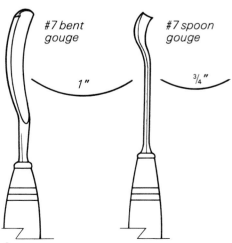

1"   #5 gouge

3/8"   #7 gouge

1"

3/8"   #8 gouge

3/4"

#7 bent gouge   #7 spoon gouge

1"   3/4"

2

To do a good job, a carving tool must be sharp. How often you sharpen depends on the quality of your tools and the type of wood you're working. When a tool starts to dull, it will break, not carve, the fibers off the wood, especially when working across the grain. It's time to sharpen your tools when they stop cutting cleanly. If you don't let your tools get too dull in the first place, they will not take long to resharpen.

The techniques for sharpening carving tools are essentially the same as those for sharpening plane irons and flat chisels. I prefer to use a belt sander equipped with a fine-grit belt (nothing coarser than used, worn-out, 120-grit belts) and a buffer, though there are many different opinions on the best way to do the job.

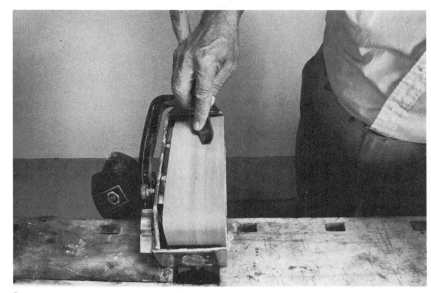

3

The cutting edge of most carving tools should be beveled to approximately 30°. Lightly hold the tool in your hand and roll it from side to side on the running sander **(3)**, making sure that you keep the tool moving. Don't let the blade get too hot or you will ruin the temper and damage the edge of the blade.

The sanding marks should be 90° to the edge of the chisel, but no less than 45°. Many people prefer to hold the tool sideways **(4)**, which is easier but wrong, because then the sanding marks will go with the bevel. A sanding mark that is right on the edge of the tool **(5)** will prevent the tool from becoming truly sharp.

When you've got a small, even burr on the back of your tool, buff the bevel until the burr is removed **(6)**.

4   **5**

6

You can also use a flat stone to sharpen carving tools **(7)**. Be sure to work over the whole surface of the stone so you don't get a hollow spot in any one place. Sharpen as you would on the belt sander until the edge has a small burr on the back.

To remove the burr, you will need a stone that fits the shape of the back of the gouge. Here are a few of the stone shapes that are available **(8)**. The most commonly used is the gouge slipstone **(9)**. It is concave on one side, convex on the other and tapered, so you can usually find some place on the stone that will fit the tool **(10,11)**. With the stone in hand, remove the burr from the gouge, being careful not to bevel the back edge. ☐

7

8

9

10

11

Carving a Bowl

Draw the shape of the inside of the bowl on the wood **(1)** before cutting into it. How you orient the bowl on the wood depends on the type of grain you want the bowl to have. If positioned as shown here **(2)**, the grain will be very strong, with the annual rings cut at a great angle. Oriented like this **(3)**, the grain will be straight, since the rings will be cut at about 90°.

Carving and sanding on the inside of a bowl should always be completed before work on the outside is begun, because the work is much more easily clamped in a vise when it is still a block. As you start to carve, work either across the grain or at an angle to it. Don't go with the grain **(4)**, because you won't have much control, and the wood might split and run in any direction. For the best control, use a deep gouge **(5)**. A gouge that is too flat will split the wood, as will one the full width of the cut to be made. When starting, use a mallet to strike the gouge.

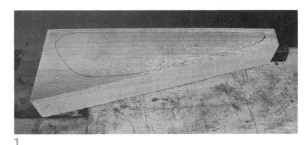

1

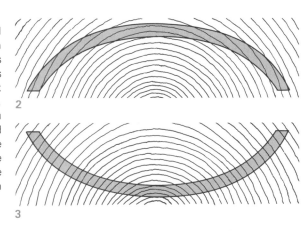

2

3

4

5

6   7

To speed up roughing out, drill holes with a Forstner bit approximately to the depth of the inside of the bowl **(6)**. A Forstner bit has a very short point **(7)** and is used where a clean, flat-bottomed hole is needed. With the holes drilled, you can carve in from any direction without splitting the wood, as long as you carve toward a deeper part of the bowl **(8)**. Carving uphill will result in loss of control, and the wood will split.

When roughing out is complete, switch to shallower gouges that approximate the shape of the bowl you want to produce. Instead of a mallet, use the weight of your body to force the gouge down. This is more difficult to explain than it is to do: Your right hand will push down on the gouge while your left hand will hold it back. If the gouge slips, the left hand will prevent it from causing any damage. In other words, your left hand acts as a pivot or an anchor, while your right hand directs the tool. For example, if you want to make the side of a bowl concave toward the bottom, let the bevel of the gouge slide on the wood being cut **(9)**, then slowly move your right hand down **(10)**. After you slip a few times, you will learn to control your tools. As you carve, don't try to steady the work with your left hand — keep both hands behind the tool edge so you will have no chance to cut yourself.

8

9   10

For cutting out the center of the bowl, where the cut angles from the bowl's top toward its lower part, use a gouge and cut with the grain **(11)**. As you carve, keep moving your hand over the work to feel for high and low spots that you might not see **(12)**.

After final carving is done, you're ready to smooth out the inside, unless you want to leave a textured surface. Sometimes I like to leave the gouge marks on the wood, as in this piece **(13)**, which is smooth on the outside and textured on the inside.   □

11

12

13

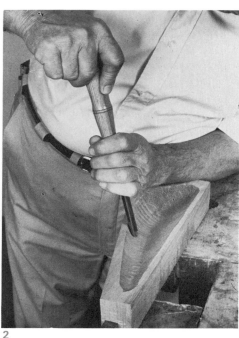

Textured Surfaces

If you want to carve a textured surface, here are two ways. Starting the gouge at the top of the bowl **(1)** and letting the bevel of the tool slide down the side of the bowl to the bottom **(2,3)** will give you a sweeping cut as on the left side of the bowl in this photo **(4)**. As you slide down, move the tool handle back to control the shape.

For a fishscale effect, as on the end of the bowl in the photo, start to carve from the bottom **(5)**. Then slide up the wood on the tool bevel as you move the handle back **(6)**. Move up the bowl wall and repeat.

Sometimes combinations of different gouges and techniques can be quite effective. Make sure you work with sharp tools when carving a textured surface, because you won't be able to rely on sanding to correct marks left by dull tools. ☐

1

2

3

4

5

6

Smoothing Out

If you choose an untextured surface, start the smoothing process by using carver burrs in a portable electric router. Here are a few examples of the different shapes available **(1)**. Smaller, more flexible tools are also available for smoothing, but I have found that the router works fine.

Hold the router firmly and don't take off too much wood at one time. Whenever possible, rest your hand against something or let one of your fingers slide against the edge of the bowl **(2)**, for guidance and safety.

The router works fast but takes skill and care to use. A slower but safer tool is a wood riffler. A riffler is a curved, half-round rasp at one end and a curved, half-round file at the other **(3)**. Rifflers, like carver burrs, are available in several different shapes. I have found the half-round shape best for my work, as there is usually a place on the tool that will fit the work **(4)**.

Use the carver burrs and router, a riffler or a combination to remove the gouge marks.

1

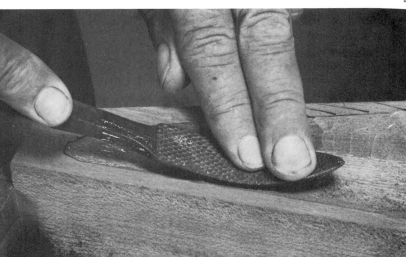

2

3

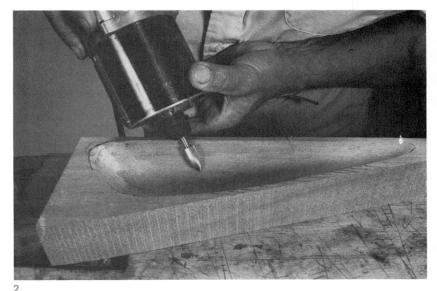

4

5

Next remove the marks left by the router or riffler. A gooseneck scraper blade is the best tool for this job **(5)**. This is an oddly shaped piece of steel that cuts with a burr on its edge. Because of its shape, there will always be some part of the curve that will fit your bowl **(6)**. Scrape with the grain until the surface is clean. (For more information on scrapers and how to sharpen them, see chapter 2.)

The final step is sanding first with medium and then fine-grit paper. Very little sanding will be necessary after scraping.

A chalkboard eraser made out of felt strips makes an excellent sanding block **(7)**. It will conform to the shape of the inside of the bowl and save the ends of your fingers. □

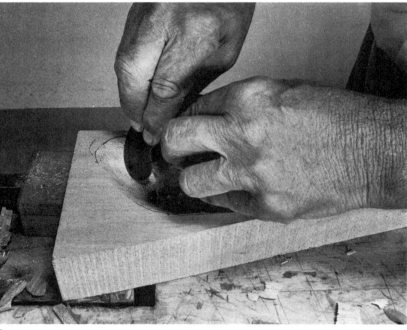

6

7

Carving the Outside

Carving the outside of the bowl can be done in several ways. I prefer to start by roughing out the shape with a bandsaw and a chisel.

First draw the shape you desire on the outside of the bowl **(1)**. Notice that the walls of the bowl are not the same thickness all around; it is not necessary to make them uniform. The appearance of a bowl can sometimes be made more interesting by varying wall thickness, which results in different but related shapes on the inside and outside.

Tilt the bandsaw table to an angle that approximates the angle on the inside of the bowl **(2)**. You can do this by eye. Then bandsaw out one side **(3)**. Next, cut both ends **(4,5)** and, finally, the last side **(6)**. Because the angles on the inside of a bowl aren't always the same, the table will usually have to be set differently for each cut.

1

2

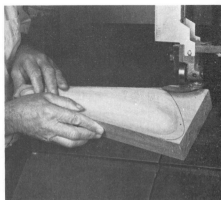

3

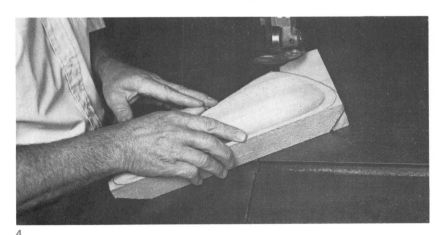

4

5

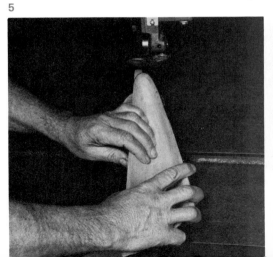

6

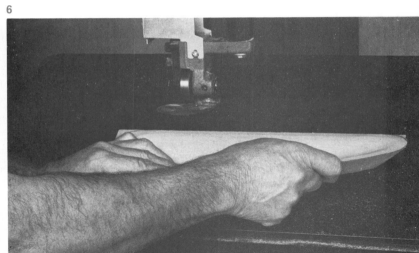

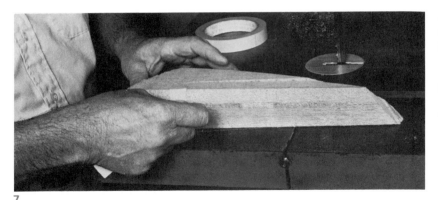

7

Save the scrap from the last cut **(7)**. You will need it to tape back on the bowl, to keep the bowl square on the table **(8)**.

Now mark the shape of the bottom of the bowl and bandsaw it out **(9)**. Once you've roughly shaped the bowl on the outside **(10)**, you're ready to start in with hand tools.

8

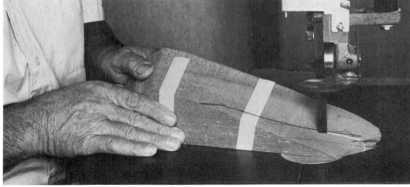

9

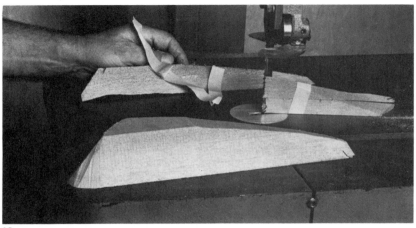

10

By planing, filing, sanding and spokeshaving, finish the top edge of the bowl first **(11,12)**. Working with the bowl resting on this edge later will help you know what shape you're working toward. Sand the surface with 80-grit sandpaper when it is the right shape **(13)**. With the top edge finished **(14)**, the rest of the outside of the bowl is ready for shaping.

11

12

13

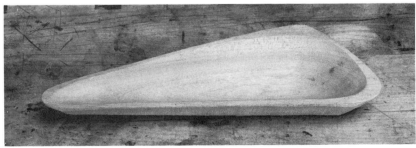

14

15

16

Clamp the bowl to the bench, letting the part being cut hang over the edge wherever possible so that you can feel the thickness of the walls. If this isn't possible, be sure to have some scrap wood underneath the bowl so you don't carve into the bench. Use a chisel to rough out the part of the bowl with end grain **(15)**.

Continually check wall thickness as you work **(16)**, being careful not to cut through. Also watch for tear-out as you work near the top edge. When the thickness of the walls seems right, begin the smoothing process. ☐

Smoothing the Outside

For smoothing you can use a router with carver burrs; a Surform, rasp and file; a block plane and spokeshave; or a combination of any or all of these tools.

A Surform **(1)** is like a rasp with holes in the teeth. The chips go through the holes so the Surform won't clog up. It works fast, stays sharp for a long time and is inexpensive. Surforms are sold in several shapes and sizes; the one that takes both a flat and half-round blade is the best for my work.

A rasp is similar to a Surform but a much older style of tool **(2)**. The rasp usually has finer teeth and, of course, no holes. It tends to clog when used on soft wood, but on hard wood it gives a nice, smooth surface. I use half-round and round patternmaker's rasps.

Wood files are just like rasps except their teeth are continuous and run at a slight angle across the width **(3)**. Some files are double cut, which means that there are two rows of teeth running at angles to one another. I use two wood files about the same shape as my rasps, but they give a much finer cut.

Clean the teeth of rasps and files with a file card. File cards are small brushes with wire on one side and bristles on the other **(4)**. Brush the teeth with the wire side first and then the bristle side.

A good way to clean a rasp or a file is to put a little alcohol on one side and light it with a match. The shavings clogging the teeth will absorb the alcohol and burn up without hurting the steel. Then you can use the file card to remove the ashes. Be careful to do this in a safe place.

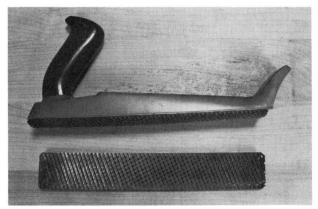

1

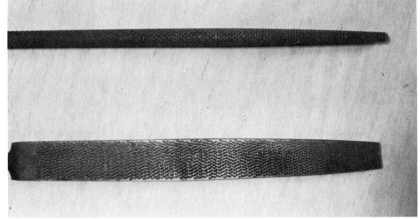

2

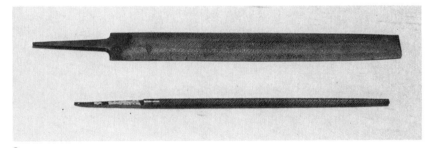

3

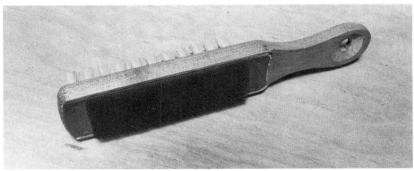

4

5

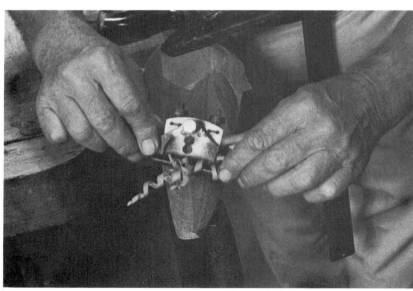

6

A block plane **(5)** is an excellent tool to use if the bowl has some straight or slightly rounded parts on the outside.

Spokeshaves can be used on many shapes **(6)** and are available in many designs: This one **(7)** is straight with a flat sole and is the one I use most. I also have one with a round sole **(8)** for concave work. I prefer spokeshaves with adjustable blade screws.

7

8

Spokeshave handles fit the palms of your hands and have two indentations for your thumbs; hold the spokeshave with those **(9)**. To avoid chattering, push the spokeshave instead of pulling it. Some spokeshaves have one handle in the front for pulling, but these are designed for rough work.

If you have difficulty holding the blade for sharpening because it is too small, make a handle for it as you would for a cabinet-scraper blade.

I begin smoothing with a Surform **(10)**, and next use a rasp and file **(11)**. On long grain, work in any angle, but on end grain, always work in the direction of the grain.

9

10

11

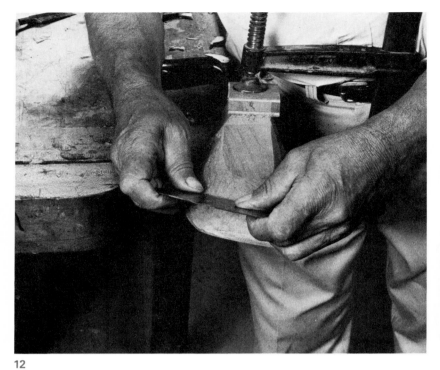

12

The two final smoothing steps, as when working on the inside of the bowl, are scraping **(12)** and sanding **(13)**. Again, a chalkboard eraser helps in sanding.

Now the bowl is sanded smooth and ready to be finished **(14)**.   □

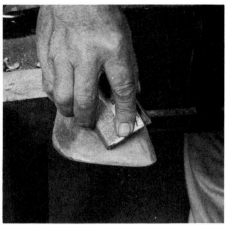

13

14

Spindle Turning

Chapter 4

Types of Turning

The woodturning lathe is the oldest of woodworking machines and the only one in which the work rather than the tool is driven by power. Skill is more important in turning than in any other machine process, although a beginner can do adequate work.

Woodturning traditionally was a trade in itself. Today woodworkers are rarely so specialized and are expected to be proficient in most areas of the craft, including turning. In this chapter, I will cover the basics only, for discussing the subject in depth could easily take a whole book.

There are two basic types of woodturning. In spindle turning the work is supported at both ends and driven at one. This is the method used for making round or partly round chair legs, table legs and other similar shapes. In faceplate turning, the method used to make bowls and round boxes, the work revolves on a faceplate secured only to the headstock of the lathe. Occasionally the two types of turning are combined.   □

The Lathe

Lathe size is determined by the maximum diameter of the work that may be turned. Therefore, a 12-in. lathe will measure 6 in. from the center of a spindle to the lathe bed. A lathe of this size will usually take spindles up to 3 ft. long.

A ¾-HP motor will furnish enough power for a 12-in. lathe, but a 1-HP motor is better. A motor with a speed of 1725 RPM used with a four-step pulley on the headstock typically will give the lathe a range of speeds from 900 to 3200 RPM, depending on the size of the pulleys. I prefer machines equipped with a four-step pulley because they experience less belt slippage and speed loss than some other types. For example, lathes having a belt with expansion pulleys for speed variation tend to have problems with slippage and slowdown, although they are safe and easy to use.

If you are serious about turning, consider a lathe that has direct drive with a variable-speed motor. These are safe and good, although they can be expensive.

Here is a typical lathe **(1)**. The headstock, driven by the motor, is to the left of the lathe. (The headstock is considered a live center because it always spins with the work.) This headstock is equipped with faceplates for both inboard and outboard turning (p. 85). The gap in the bed next to the headstock allows inboard turning of thin objects of large diameter. The tailstock is to the right. It moves along the lathe bed to accommodate work of varying lengths.

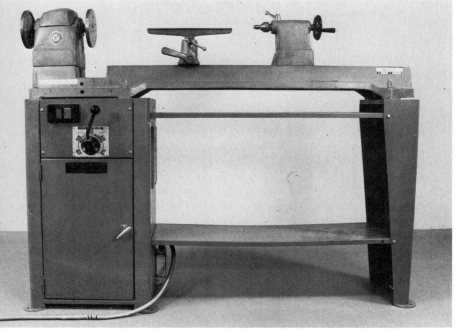

1

A spur center inserted into the headstock drives the wood for spindle turning (**2**). New lathes are usually furnished with a stationary cup center, or dead center, for the tailstock (**3,4**). The friction created between the spinning wood and the stationary cup center, however, causes a buildup of heat that can burn the wood. To prevent this, apply a coat of wax to the end of the wood. Many people use oil for this purpose, but the oil is absorbed by the wood and does not do the job as well as wax.

To avoid the problem altogether, buy a ball-bearing live center for the tailstock. Here (**5**) are three interchangeable centers that fit into a ball-bearing live center. The one inserted into the ball bearing is the cup center, which is used for turning wood. The point center is for turning metal or plastic. The flat center is for holding wood or any other material that should not be marked, such as the lid for a box during finish-turning. A live center for the tailstock is definitely a worthwhile investment.

2

3

4

5

6

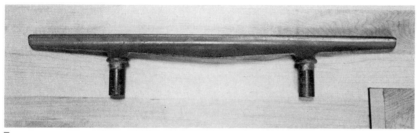

7

The tool rest is a very important part of a lathe. There are different lengths of straight tool rests available, and it is a good idea to have more than one **(6)**. Extra-long tool rests require two bases **(7)** and although they are often helpful, I don't think they are necessary except for production work.

The tool rest clamps into a base that slides along the bed of the lathe **(8)**. Position the tool rest with its top edge below the centerline of the spindle so the tool will be cutting at the centerline **(9)**. The corners of the wood should clear the tool rest by about ½ in. Always check to make sure that the wood will clear before you turn on the lathe. Here **(10)** the tool rest is too close to the work and damage could result.

If you are turning a large piece that is off balance, start the lathe at a slow speed and work the piece until it is balanced. I usually turn an average-size spindle like the one shown, which measures 2 in. by 2 in., at a speed of about 2000 RPM.

As with all woodworking operations, safety must come first in turning. Be sure you don't have any loose clothing, jewelry or hair that could get caught in the lathe. Long sleeves can be dangerous — roll them up. □

8

10

9

Mounting the Work

Some people prefer to cut the corners off a turning blank so that it is octagonal before they put it on the lathe **(1)**. I find it faster to cut off the corners on the lathe. On pieces too big to clear the bed, however, I cut off the corners first on a table saw or a bandsaw.

To mount a piece of wood between centers for spindle turning, first find the exact center of the piece of wood. Do this by drawing two diagonal lines from corner to corner on each end **(2)**. Use an awl to make a hole in the tailstock end of the piece of wood where the two lines cross. In the headstock end, make two diagonal saw cuts **(3)** with a handsaw. This will make it possible for the spur center to grip the wood and spin it.

Drive the spur center into the saw cuts with a mallet **(4)**.

To secure the wood in the lathe, insert the end with the spur center into the headstock first, then move the tailstock up to the other end and clamp it tightly. Turn the handle on the tailstock until the point of the cup center engages the center hole in the wood. Keep turning the handle until the rim of the cup cuts into the wood. The cup center should be tight against the wood at all times, but not so tight that the work won't turn freely.

Make sure to lock the tailstock with its clamp **(5)** so that the vibrations won't work it loose. During turning, occasionally check that the cup is still tight against the work.   ☐

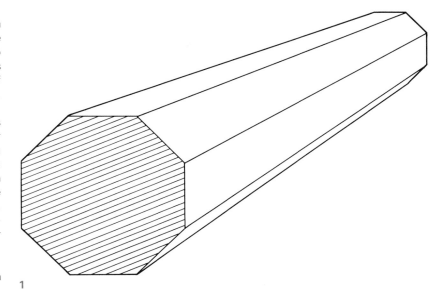

1

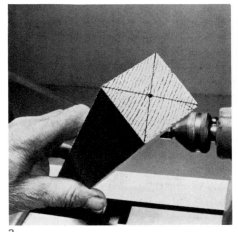

2

3

4

5

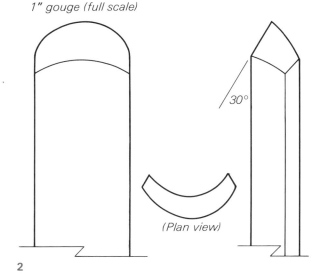

1

1" gouge (full scale)

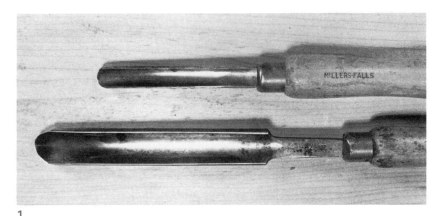

30°

(Plan view)

2

Tools

Turning tools are usually sold in sets, but they can also be bought individually, or made. For spindle turning, I use a gouge, a parting tool and a skew. A beginner should have at least four tools to start: ½-in. and 1-in. gouges, a parting tool and a 1-in. skew.

Gouges **(1,2)** come in different sizes and are used primarily for roughing out the work and for cutting coves. Some skilled turners also use a gouge for faceplate turning, but this takes a lot of skill and I don't recommend it for beginners. I will discuss parting tools and skews as they are used.

In general, turning technique is similar to carving technique, but instead of hitting your tools with a mallet, the spinning of the wood supplies the hitting power. ☐

Roughing Out a Cylinder

To rough out a cylinder, first rest a 1-in. gouge against the tool rest **(1)**, and then slowly and carefully move the cutting edge up into the spinning wood. Always approach the wood in this manner—if you move the tool downward into the wood, there's a good chance that the tool will catch and break either itself or the tool rest. That is an easy way to get hurt.

If you start into the wood with the gouge from the end or in the center, you have little control over the wood splitting. Here **(2,3)** the tool is on top of the piece of wood just to make that point—your tool should always be on the tool rest.

1

2

3

To prevent the wood from splitting, approach the work as though it were a pencil and you were trying to sharpen it with a gouge (4). Continue like that, until the corners are removed and the piece is fairly round. Then let your finger and the tool slide along the tool rest (5,6), until the piece is completely round. You don't have to stop the lathe each time to check if the piece is round. After you have some experience, you can simply rest the center part of the back of the gouge lightly on the wood while it is spinning (7). If the wood is round, there will be no noise, but if there are still a few flat spots, the tool will bounce audibly. Of course, you shouldn't try this when the wood is still square.

With one end of the spindle rounded, shut off the lathe, move the tool rest over to the other end and continue turning. Use the gouge in the opposite direction without changing hands. Get used to using the tools in both directions because this will help you to do more consistent work.   □

4

5

6

7

Dimensioning a Cylinder

When you think the cylinder is round and has no flat spots, make it the same diameter along its entire length. For this you'll need a parting tool and an outside caliper.

A parting tool **(1,2)** is used in general for cutting grooves and in particular for dimensioning and marking the spindles to length. The best parting tools are thicker in the center than they are at the edges and thus they clear the sides of the groove they cut. This prevents the tool from heating up and becoming damaged and from burning the wood. All parting tools are available in thicknesses of ⅛ in. and ¼ in. I prefer a ⅛-in. parting tool.

An outside caliper **(3)** is used to measure thickness and outside dimensions.

To dimension the cylinder, hold the parting tool in the right hand at 90° to the tool rest. Set the caliper to the desired diameter (plus a little extra to allow for finish-turning and sanding) and hold it in the left hand. With the lathe running, move the parting tool into the wood and let the caliper rest in the groove until it slips on **(4)**. Then stop cutting and pull the caliper off that spot.

In this manner make several grooves along the length of the cylinder. Remember to make sure that the cylinder has no flat spots before doing any of this, because the caliper will get caught on these.

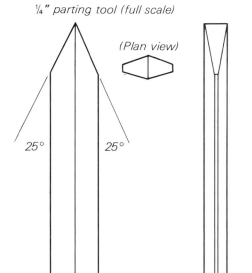

¼" parting tool (full scale)

(Plan view)

25°   25°

1

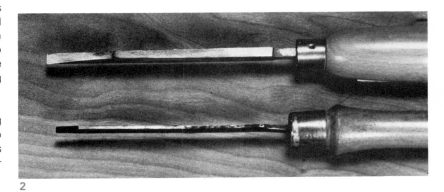

2

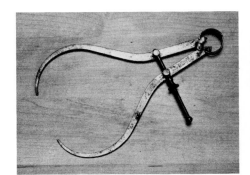

3

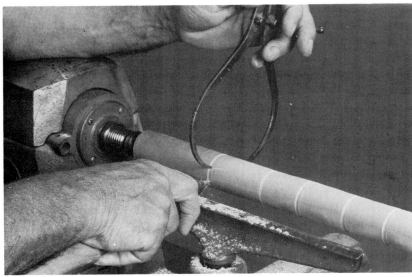

4

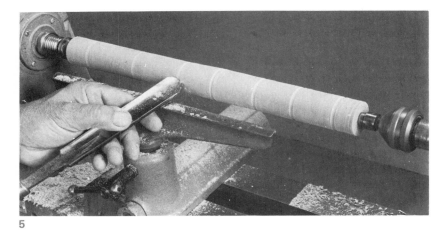

5

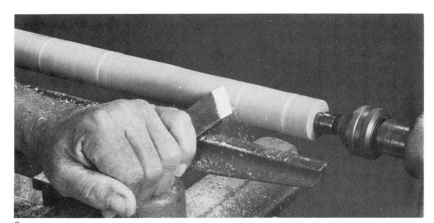

6

7

Remove the wood between the grooves with a gouge **(5)**. Finish off with a skew **(6)**.

The skew **(7)** works like a smoothing plane, but unlike a plane's edge, the cutting edge of a skew is sharpened on both sides **(8)**. Skews are available in different widths and are also used for cutting some *V*-grooves and for making rings and beads.

1" skew (full scale)

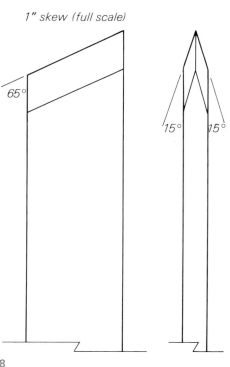

8

The skew is an important lathe tool but very difficult to learn how to use properly. First of all, watch out for that top corner — if it catches, the work is ruined **(9)**.

To use a skew correctly, be sure that its bevel rests against the cylinder **(10)**. Then slowly move the skew into the work by raising the handle. If the skew bevel doesn't rest on the work when you're starting **(11)**, it will definitely dig right in. Once you've gotten off to a safe start, you can move the tool from the center of the cylinder toward the ends.

9

10

11

12

13

14

15

Here **(12,13)** I am going from the center to the left. Notice that I hold the end of the skew in my right hand against my hip. In the beginning, it's a good idea to do it this way, although when you are more experienced, you shouldn't have to. Without moving your feet, move your upper body and hips toward the left.

Here **(14,15)** I am moving from the center to the right. Notice that here again I don't change the position of my feet, but instead I move my hips and upper body.

Be sure to cut with the middle of the cutting edge **(16)**. Watch out for that top corner. ☐

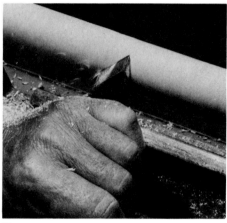

16

A Dimensioning Jig

For a precise cylinder, use a plane with a jig made for the lathe **(1)**. When the jig is placed on the lathe upside-down, you can see that it is made like a miter box **(2)**. The piece that is nailed and glued to the bottom fits snugly into the groove in the lathe bed **(3)**. Notice the blocks with *T*-nuts are positioned to slide through the groove. When the box is in place, turn the blocks to secure the box to the bed.

The rough-turned cylinder is mounted between the headstock and the tailstock, inside the box **(4)**.

With the lathe running at slow speed, rest the plane on top of the box and shave off a small amount of wood until the plane won't cut anymore **(5)**.

You can build the jig so that its sides adjust to accept work of different diameters, but I have found it is better to screw the box together at one size and then drill new screw holes as necessary. □

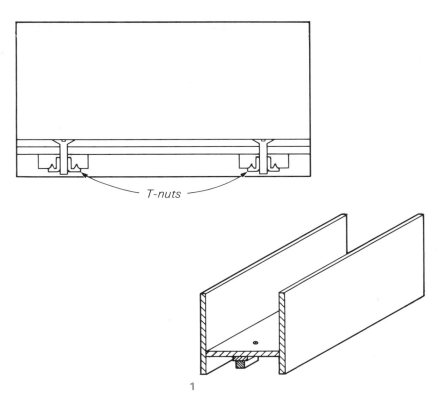

T-nuts

1

2

4

3

5

Scraping Versus Carving

There are two techniques used in spindle turning. Scraping is the method used by most beginners. Carving is the method used by skilled turners. Carving requires skill, experience and practice, but it is well worth learning from the beginning because you'll save lots of time in the long run.

Here is a brief description of the differences between the two methods:

Scraping is the easy way to turn — just rest the tool at 90° to the tool rest and scrape the wood **(1,2)**. The shavings fly right at your face because in scraping, the fibers of the wood are pulled off, not cut off.

In carving, the tool is tilted and held at an angle to the work. Shavings will not fly up into your face with this technique. Explaining the correct angle at which to hold the tool is impossible. To learn the right way, stop the lathe, put your tool on the tool rest and experiment, using your tool the way you would use a carving chisel. The way that allows the cleanest cut is the best way to hold the tool. Now start the lathe and work. You will find that the tool cuts beautifully **(3)**.

Here is the difference between scraped and carved wood **(4)**. The left side is carved and the right side is scraped. The work could be sanded so that both sides are smooth, but the minute the finish was put on, the fibers on the scraped surface would raise.

1

2

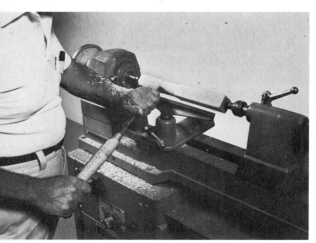

3

4

Here is another example **(5)**. Notice how sharp and clean the carved cut is on this ring. The same shape scraped on the same piece of wood is fuzzy and rough **(6)**.

Here's a cove cut that has been carved **(7)** and one that has been scraped **(8)**. When carving a cove, carve halfway down from each side so that you will always be cutting with the grain **(9,10)**.

5

6

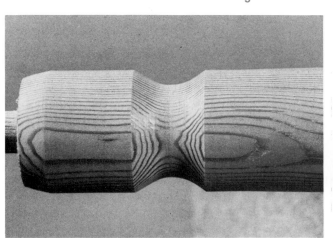

7

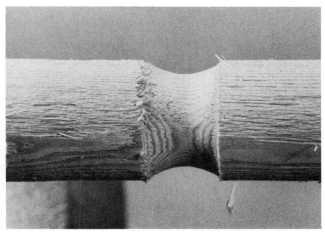

8

9

10

11

12

To carve a *V*-cut, use the upper point of a skew. Hold it 90° to the tool rest **(11)**. This is the only time you should use the point of the skew. For rounding off the end grain, use the lower corner of the skew **(12)**, and as you carve, roll it.

When turning from a rectangular section into a round **(13)**, use a skew. First make a *V*-cut with the upper corner **(14)**. Then, using the lower corner, roll the skew as you cut **(15,16,17)**. □

13

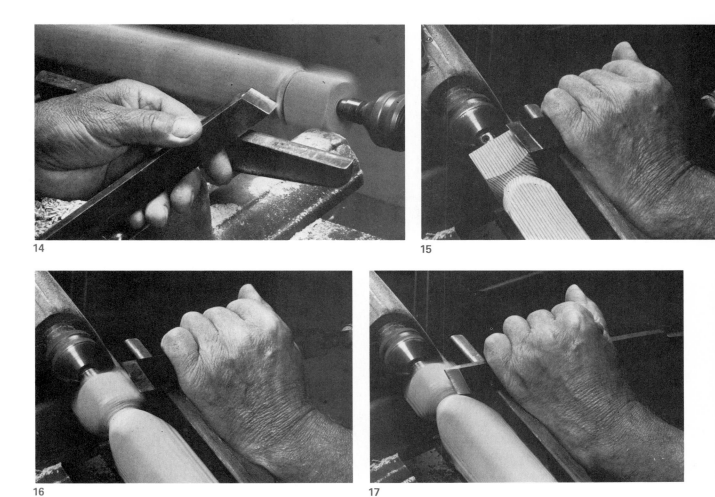

14

15

16

17

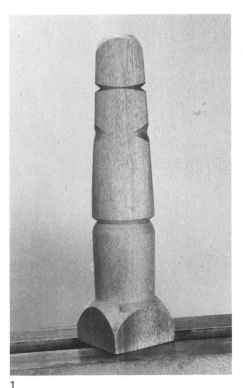

1

Off-Center and Half-Round Turning

Spindle turnings do not always have to be round in section. By offsetting the centers, it is possible to turn a wide range of shapes such as ovals, triangles and even rounded squares. Here **(1)** is a spindle that is square on one end, round in the middle and triangular on the other end. These techniques require some practice, so it's best to make sure that you are in complete control of your tools before trying off-center turning.

To turn a piece that is round on one end and triangular on the other, first make a full-scale drawing **(2)** of the end of the piece of wood you will be using, in order to locate the points for the cup center. Then transfer the markings to the wood. Turn it as a cylinder and sand.

Insert the cup center into one of the points of the triangle **(3)**. Before starting the lathe, rotate the piece by hand to make sure it clears the tool rest.

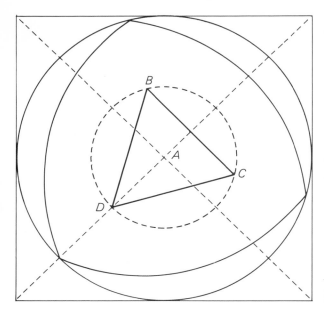

A, center for cylinder
B, C, D, centers for triangle

2

3

For this operation, use only a gouge **(4,5)**. Do not use a skew because it will catch. Turn the wood as cleanly as possible. Repeat the procedure until you have used all of the points to turn the wood. Here is the turned piece **(6)**.

When sanding an off-center piece, always use a sanding block. I find that a piece of cork (p. 175) makes a good block.

You can also make identical half rounds or quarter rounds easily by spindle turning.

To make half rounds, glue two pieces of wood together with brown paper between them using hot glue **(7)**. If you use a slow-drying glue, the paper will absorb some of the glue and the pieces will not separate later. Don't put too much glue on and don't use glue so thin that it will penetrate the paper. Don't use newspaper, because the glue will go right through it. The pieces should not be clamped — by pressing them together with your hands you can give just the right amount of pressure.

As a safety precaution, make the pieces longer than you need and either put a screw in each end or wire them together as I have done here **(8)**. Making a saw cut or a groove for the wire helps prevent it from slipping. With the ends bound this way, the pieces won't fly apart even if the glue joint fails.

Another good safety precaution is to cut the corners off the piece after it is glued up, so that it becomes an octagon.

4

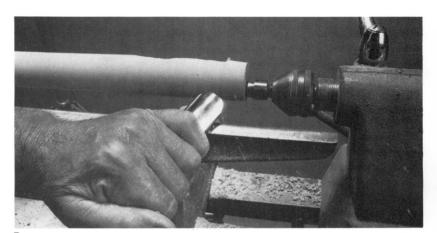

5

7

6

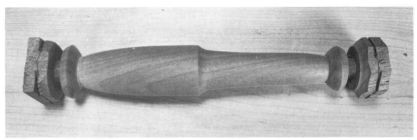

8

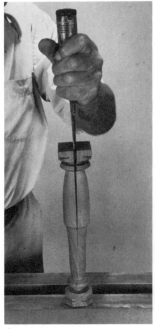

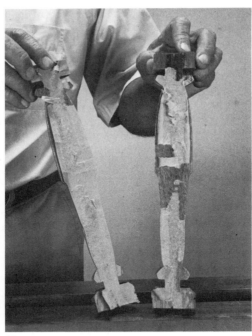

9   10

After you've turned and sanded the piece, split it apart with a chisel **(9,10)**. Cut the ends off, and the turnings are complete **(11)**.

A few final pointers on spindle turning: Whenever possible, make any joints or holes in the wood before you turn it. The holes will not interfere with the turning; just be careful when you sand the work, and use a sanding block if you can.

If there are to be any square sections on the spindle, pencil them out carefully on all four sides before you begin turning **(12)**.

If any saw cuts have to be made on the piece after it is turned, try to leave the ends square for reference **(13)**.   □

11

12

13

Sanding

Most of the time you will need to sand the work you have turned. This is easiest while the work is still on the lathe.

Before you start to sand, always remove the tool rest so your fingers won't get caught between it and the turning work **(1)**.

For better control of the sandpaper, fold it over three times so that it won't slide **(2,3)**. Sandpaper folded this way can easily be formed into certain shapes **(4)**.

1

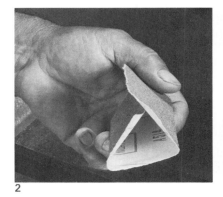

2

3

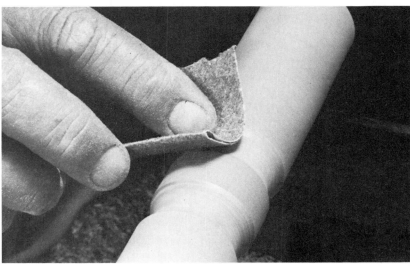

4

5

When you are sanding a straight cylinder, a blackboard eraser makes a fine sanding block because it has just the right amount of flexibility **(5)**. But always use a regular sanding block when you are sanding an off-center piece **(6)**. Sanding blocks, however, are often not suitable for what you need to do, so you will have to use your fingers sometimes. The most important thing to remember is to be careful. For example, when sanding a piece that goes from square to round, don't put on pressure with your fingers in the center of the sandpaper. Keep your hands out on the end **(7,8)** so that your fingers won't get cut by the sharp corners. By the way, it's a very good idea to wear gloves when sanding. □

6

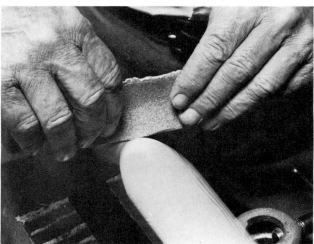

7

8

Faceplate Turning
Chapter 5

Mounting the Work

1

Only the headstock of the lathe is used in faceplate turning, although sometimes, if the wood is off balance or heavy, or when turning without a scrap plate, the tailstock is used to support the work temporarily. A faceplate **(1)** is a steel disc that threads onto the headstock. All faceplates have threads going in a direction opposite to the spinning of the motor so that they will not come loose while the lathe is running. Faceplates for in-board turning are thus threaded differently than those for outboard turning. Some faceplates have double threads so that they can be used both inboard and outboard.

Faceplates have holes in them through which the turning blank can be screwed, but most people screw the faceplate to a plate of scrap wood that is glued to the bottom of the turning blank. The scrap plate allows you to make full use of the wood to get a deeper bowl, as well as to avoid having screw holes in the work. Always make the scrap plate about ½ in. larger than the diameter of the faceplate — screws too close to the edge might split the wood. Cut the plate round on a bandsaw or with a sabersaw, or at least cut off the corners and make it octagonal. Do this also to the turning blank. Square corners are dangerous.

To make sure the work will be perfectly centered, use the center mark of the scrap plate, which is glued to the square block to be turned, to draw out the bowl **(2)**. I suggest beginners glue the scrap plate directly to the turning blank with Titebond and then cut or chisel the plate off after turning. More experienced turners can glue a piece of brown paper between the plate and the blank so that the two will separate easily after turning. I discuss this technique and other ways to mount the work later in this chapter.

When the scrap plate has been glued to the turning blank and the faceplate is screwed onto it **(3)**, you're ready to thread the assembly onto the headstock. If you like, you can center the work at this point instead of earlier: Mount the assembly on the lathe and spin it by hand while marking out the bowl with a pencil held securely on the tool rest. Then unscrew the assembly from the headstock and bandsaw out the bowl.

When mounting the faceplate to the lathe, make sure to screw it on securely. Most lathe motors have a brake on them and, with the motor stopping and the spinning piece of wood acting like a flywheel, the wood will continue spinning until it unscrews itself and flies off. This is particularly a problem when working with large pieces outboard. □

2

3

Tools

Faceplate turning takes less skill than spindle turning because it is done mostly by scraping — the tool has to cut both with and across the grain. For tools I use diamond-point and round-nose chisels, which are designed for faceplate turning only **(1)**. Some professional turners use gouges for faceplate turning, but before you do this you'd better get proper instruction. I tried this a few times and almost killed myself.

Because diamond-point and round-nose chisels are designed for scraping, I don't hone them but leave on the burr, which is the actual cutting edge, as on a scraper blade. The chisels cut better this way. Many people use these tools for spindle turning because they are easy to use. The result is that the wood needs much more sanding afterward, and the cut is neither accurate nor controlled.

Most available diamond-point and round-nose chisels are made from too-thin steel that bends easily if caught in the wood **(2)**. Tools made from this steel also vibrate when used to make deep cuts where the tool rest can't reach, as when cutting the inside of a deep bowl. My students and I make our own tools out of 18-ft. lengths of unhardened ½-in. by ½-in. oil-hardening steel. We cut the lengths to about 15 in., grind them to shape and then send them out to be hardened. Finally, we turn the handles. Excellent 12-in. long-and-strong tools are the result **(3)**. (If you plan to turn much abrasive wood, such as teak or rosewood, you might consider investing in carbide-tipped tools.)

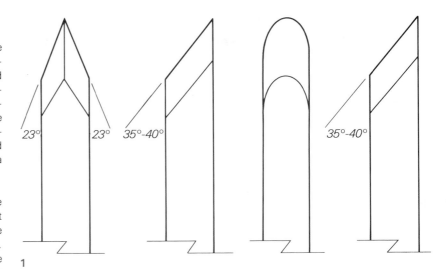

1

2

3

4

Use a diamond-point chisel to shape the outside of most bowls; use a round-nose chisel for bowls having coves or cavities. Set your tool rest so that the point of the chisel is right in the center of the bowl **(4)** when the tool is held 90° to the rest **(5)**. This is the correct way to hold both diamond-point and round-nose chisels. You can tilt the handle up a little **(6)**, but never hold it as you would a gouge or a skew **(7)**. If you do, the tool will dig right in, which results in either a split bowl, a broken tool rest or a bent chisel.

In these photos I am using a right-angle tool rest, which does not have to be readjusted for outside and inside turning when making small bowls. One of these is not really necessary unless you plan to make a large number of small bowls or plates. □

5

6

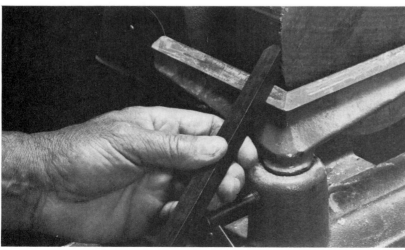

7

Turning a Bowl

As in spindle turning, start faceplate turning slowly. First, balance the work at slow speed. The larger the piece you are turning, the slower the lathe speed should be. At any given speed, the outside edge of a larger circle of wood will move into your tool faster than that of a smaller piece of wood.

Use only the tip of the diamond-point chisel for scraping **(1)**, and make sure the back of the chisel sits flat on the tool rest. Do the same when using the round nose. When the outside is perfectly round, true up the top of the bowl **(2)**. Then step up the speed and shape the outside of the bowl **(3)**. For the final cut, run the lathe at high speed, about 1500 RPM, depending on the size of the bowl. Take a very fine cut so there will be little sanding to do. If much sanding is necessary, the bowl might end up oval. The sides of the bowl are made up of both long grain and end grain, and of course end grain won't sand as fast as long grain.

To sand, remove the tool rest and run the lathe at about half the speed of the final cut. Use coarse paper first, about 60 grit, and then sand through 80 grit, 120 grit and 180 grit to smooth out the scratches **(4,5)**. Finish with 220 grit. Keep moving the sandpaper back and forth to prevent deep scratches.

1

2

3

4

5

6

7

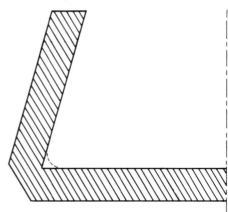

8

Now you are ready to turn the inside. This is usually done with a round-nose chisel, but you might need to use a diamond-point, depending on the shape you desire. The techniques for inside turning **(6,7)** are the same as for outside turning, but here are a few tips.

When turning the inside of a bowl, try to avoid having the sides and the bottom meet in a sharp corner **(8)**, for this shape is very difficult to sand. Try instead to have the sides and the bottom meet as shown by the dotted line.

Keep track of the depth of the bowl as you work, stopping the lathe occasionally to check it **(9)**. Don't try to make a bowl 2⅛ in. deep with stock that's only 2 in. thick.

When turning the inside, you should always work from the outer edge to the center, to go with the grain **(10)**.

9

10

Use outside calipers to check that the sides of the bowl are the right thickness **(11)**. Use inside calipers to check that inside dimensions are correct **(12)**.

Sand the inside of the bowl the same way that you sanded the outside **(13)**. Wear gloves to protect your fingers.

If the diameter of the piece to be turned is too big for inboard turning, you'll have to turn outboard **(14)**. For that you'll need a floor stand to hold the tool rest. You will also need a faceplate with the correctly reversed thread. Techniques for outboard turning are the same as for inboard turning. Turn the outside first **(15)**, then the inside **(16)**.

Beginners should not attempt the outboard turning of pieces larger than 18 in. in diameter. Instead, work with a router rigged on an arm on a center pivot. If you do turn pieces larger than 18 in. on the lathe, make sure lathe and tool rest are secure. If necessary, brace the lathe to your shop floor, wall and ceiling.   □

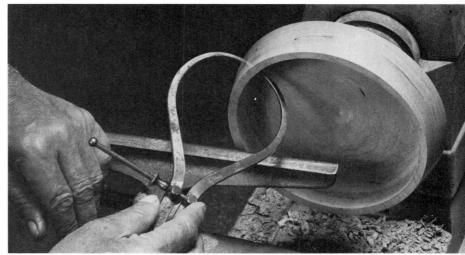

11

12

13

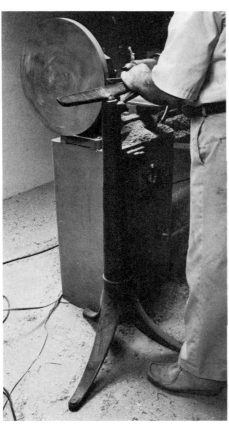

14

15

16

1   2

3

Another Way to Mount the Work

Here's a fast, easy way to make plates and small bowls without screwing the work to the faceplate. Instead, screw a piece of ¾-in. plywood to the faceplate **(1)**. Make sure it does not wobble (if it does, turn it so the surface is perfectly flat and the edge perfectly round), and then glue on a piece of 40-grit sandpaper. This will drive the work.

Plane the back of the plate to be turned and bandsaw it to the approximate shape **(2)**. Remember to mark the center on the top of the plate when drawing the circle.

Now, put the planed side against the sandpaper and move up the tailstock, into which a live cup center has been chucked, until the cup center touches the center mark on the plate **(3)**. The plate should sit firmly against the sandpaper. Be sure to lock the handle before turning on the lathe.

Switch on the lathe and turn and sand the outside and inside of the plate **(4,5)**. Of course, you cannot turn the very center of the inside because the tailstock is in the way.

4

5

When the plate is completed, remove the remaining center piece **(6)** with a Forstner bit in the drill press or with a chisel **(7)**. Smooth with a scraper blade **(8)**, and then with a sanding block and sandpaper going with the grain **(9)**.

The plate is finished **(10)**. Sign it and you can charge more if you have the right name.   □

6

7

8

9

10

1

2

3

4

Turning Bowls with Bases

If your bowl will have a foot or base, turn that first.

Screw the faceplate directly to what will be the top of the bowl **(1)**. Rough-turn the outside of the bowl, finish-turn and sand the base **(2)**, and then cut a scrap plate to glue onto the bottom of the bowl and screw a faceplate to it.

Apply a small amount of hot glue to the outside edge of the base of the bowl **(3)**. Try to avoid getting the glue on the inside edge because it will be difficult to clean off later. Apply the glue to the edge of the scrap plate, too, and put on a layer of brown paper.

Now move the tailstock up, place the faceplate in front of the live center and tighten the tailstock **(4)**. The live center is tapered and will automatically center the faceplate. To check, turn on the lathe. If the scrap plate is slightly off center, it will be able to center itself because the glue is not dry. To prevent the glue from setting up too fast, it might be a good idea to take the chill off the plate, but don't make it too hot.

Remove the bowl from the lathe after about a half hour and set it aside for curing. When the glue has cured, which takes about 24 hours, remove the faceplate that is on the top of the bowl and place the bowl back on the headstock **(5)**. For safety, move the tailstock up to prevent the bowl from flying off. Turn and sand the outside.

Turn the inside, but leave the tailstock in place until the walls are the right thickness and the bowl is the right depth **(6)**. Then remove the tailstock, turn down the center plug **(7)** and sand the inside of the bowl **(8)**.

5

6

7

8

9

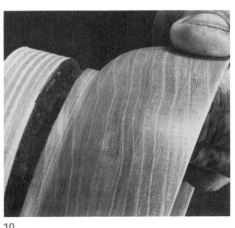

10

To remove the bowl from the scrap plate, put a chisel right in the glueline and hit it lightly until the bowl starts to separate **(9)**. Carefully pry with the chisel, and then pull the bowl off with your hand **(10,11)**.

Here the bowl and the scrap plate are separated **(12)**. Notice that the brown paper split in half. Don't use newspaper because it will absorb the glue and prevent the bowl from separating cleanly. Sand the bottom of the bowl to remove the paper and the bowl is ready to be signed and finished **(13)**. I usually use salad-bowl finish for bowls that will come in contact with food. ☐

11

12

13

Off-Center Turning

Off-center turning can be done by faceplate turning as well as spindle turning, but don't try it until you have mastered regular faceplate turning. Using a wedge between the faceplate and the wood is another, safer way to do the work and still produce some interesting shapes.

First, turn and sand the outside and rim of your bowl **(1)**. Then loosen the screws in the faceplate and insert a wedge. Remove one screw at a time, replacing each with a longer screw of the same number **(2,3)**. Put the piece back on the lathe. The piece will wobble **(4)**, so start off slowly.

Remove the high spots on the bowl and increase the speed. Continue turning until you get the desired shape **(5)**, then sand.

1

2

3

4

5

6

Here is the piece rough-sanded **(6)**. It is deeper on one side than the other, a shape that would be good for a stool seat or a platter for carving.

But the bottom has three screw holes that still have to be plugged. To do this, use a plug cutter **(7)** mounted in a drill press. You can cut across the grain to make plugs or with the grain to make dowels.

When cutting plugs, don't let the cutter go through the full thickness of the board or you'll have to stop the drill press each time and remove the plug from the cutter. It's easier to leave the plugs on the board and chisel them off later **(8)**.

Redrill the screw holes in the bottom of the bowl so that the plugs will fit snugly. Put glue in the holes and hammer in the plugs, making sure that the grain of the plugs goes in the same direction as that of the bowl **(9)**. When the glue is dry, chisel off the excess and sand the bottom of the bowl **(10)**.   □

7

8

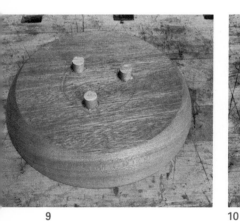

9

10

Turning Large Bowls

Stacking   Finding dry wood from which to turn bowls more than 2 in. or 3 in. deep is difficult, and if you do find some, it will be expensive. But there are several other ways to make deep bowls. You can stack them, turn them green or bricklay them.

Stacking wood for large bowls is often a great waste of materials and labor. The most common way is to glue several pieces on top of one another **(1)**. Frequently, pieces are sandwiched together with the grains at 90° to each other **(2)**. After a short time, a bowl built this way will split apart.

Here is one way to make a stacked bowl with less waste. Draw to full scale the shape of half the bowl. Draw in the thickness of the layers and mark the width of the rings. Add ⅛ in. to each side to be sure that you'll have enough wood if you find, when turning, that the bowl is a little off center **(3)**.

With a compass, take all the different radii from drawing **3** and draw the rings **(4)** onto the wood. Make them in two half circles, bandsaw them out and glue them together. Or, cut out a full ring with a jigsaw. If you do this, you could use the waste from the center to make smaller bowls. If you're making only one bowl, as is the case here, you could use the center piece from ring 1 for ring 4; ring 5 could be made from ring 2.

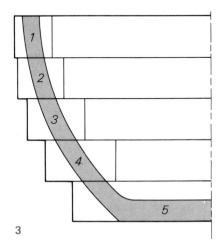

3

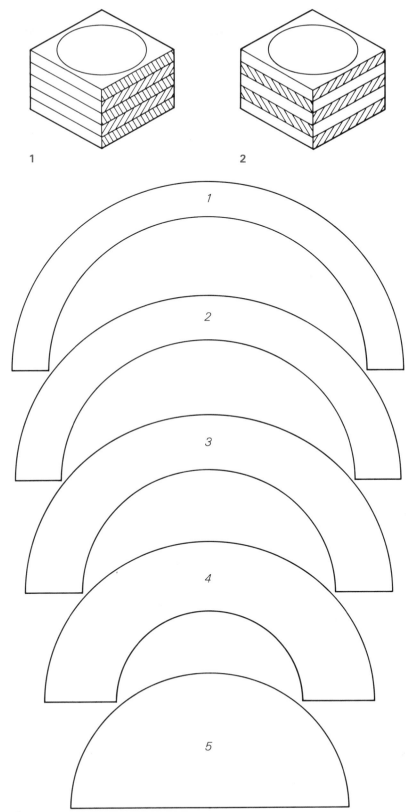

4

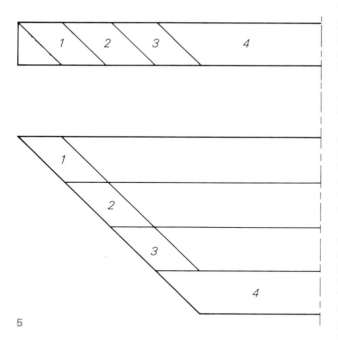

The most economical way to make a stacked bowl is to bandsaw the half rings out of two boards with the table tilted 45°. The only drawback is that very little variation of shape is possible with this method.

Again, make a full-scale drawing of half the bowl **(5)**. Then draw in the layers. Here I use 1-in. thick boards, so the width of the rings also has to be 1 in. Using 1-in. stock gives me room to shape the bowl a little. If I used 2-in. stock, the possibilities for shaping would increase, but so would the waste. If the bowl was to have straight sides, not rounded, I would use ¾-in. thick boards.

Joint the edges of the two boards you are going to use, because they will be glued together later. With the boards together **(6)**, draw the circles and bandsaw them out with the saw table tilted 45°. The only waste is the sawdust from the kerf, and the two outside pieces **(7)**. The two inside pieces will become the bottom of the bowl **(8)**.

5

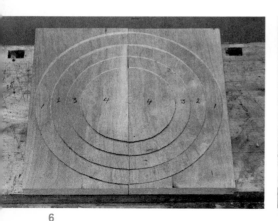

6

7

8

Now glue the pairs of half pieces together, clamping one half ring to a flat board. Don't use hot glue if the bowl will be washed in water, and place a piece of paper under the joint so it won't stick to the board. Put glue on the ends of both pieces and press them tightly together. Then put on the two other clamps **(9)**.

When the glue has dried, clean off the excess with a chisel, plane or belt sander. Then stack the rings and glue them together. Lining up the joints might look best **(10)**, but I prefer to offset the joints a little for more strength. Here **(11)** they are offset about ¾ in., not enough to make the bowl crack. An offset of 2 in. would be too much.

After stacking is complete, glue on a scrap plate to accept the faceplate. Because the base of this bowl is quite small, I would not use paper between it and the scrap plate. When turning is finished, saw the plate off.

Here's the bowl glued together, ready for turning **(12)**, and after turning **(13)**.

9

10

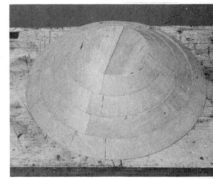

11

12

13

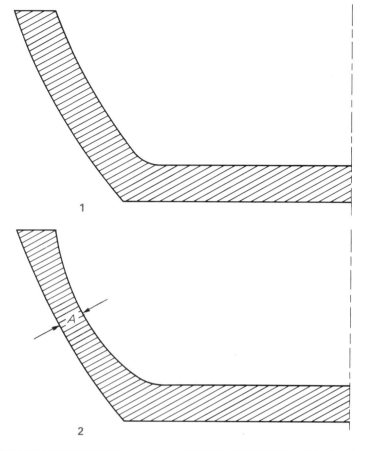

1

2

Green wood   It is easiest and fastest to turn green wood, but in between rough-turning and finish-turning the wood has to dry, and the long drying time is a disadvantage.

Green wood turns very fast and its smell is not always pleasant. Bowls turned from green wood are worked the same way as those from dry wood, with the same tools. You must, however, screw the faceplate directly to green wood, because glue will not stick to it. In addition, the walls of green-turned bowls have to be left thick because once the wood is dry the bowl will have to be finish-turned. The walls must be the same thickness all around **(1,2)** or else the thinner areas will dry faster and shrink more than the thicker ones, causing the wood to crack, especially on end grain. Remember, the log's pith will crack when it is dry, so don't try to turn a bowl out of wood containing it.

There are many opinions as to the best way to dry green-turned bowls. I store mine in an open shed so air can circulate around them. (Don't put them in the sun or they will crack.) Before storing, weigh the bowls and label each with the weight and date. Then, every week or two, depending on the size of the bowls, record the current weight. When the bowls have been the same weight for several weeks, they're probably dry. I usually take mine inside the shop for a couple of weeks before finish-turning so they'll reach equilibrium with the shop atmosphere.

Some people prefer burying green-turned bowls in sawdust to draw out the moisture. This is a good method but time-consuming.

As green bowls dry, they will shrink in both width and thickness. The bowl here **(3)** was 9 in. in diameter when turned. It still measures 9 in. going with the grain, but across the grain it is $8^{11}/_{16}$ in. wide, $^5/_{16}$ in. less **(4)**.

3

4

This bowl **(5)** was made out of half a tree trunk and measured 3½ in. tall when green. It shrank at different rates because the old wood (the heartwood) shrank less than the new (the sapwood) **(6)**. The middle of the bowl now measures 3⅜ in. **(7)** and the sides measure 3¼ in. **(8)**. Notice that the middle of the bowl, with the end grain, has the old wood, which has shrunk less than the sides with the long grain and the new wood.

The use of polyethylene glycol (PEG) is becoming more and more popular these days for stabilizing wood and preventing it from shrinking. PEG molecules replace the water molecules in wood and remain there when the wood dries, reducing dimensional change. I don't use PEG because I don't like what it does to the color of the wood.

5

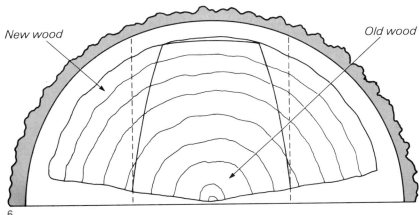

New wood   *Old wood*

6

7

8

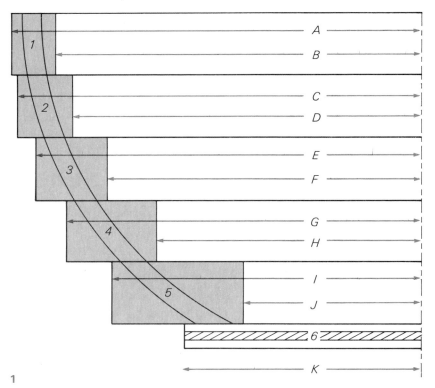

1

Bricklaying   Bricklaying is a technique that has been used for years to make such things as large wooden pulleys for belt-driven machines and frames for upholstered furniture. Patternmakers also use bricklaying to make complicated objects. It is a good way to make a stable bowl of any shape, with little waste, and can be attractive, too.

Circular bricklaying might seem difficult and complicated, but it isn't. It is more difficult to explain than it is to do. You can make the joints by hand using a miter box and a block plane, but that is time-consuming. The best and easiest way to make the joints is to use a table saw.

First, draw the shape of half the bowl from the side view in full scale, and then draw in the rings — as many as you want **(1)**. Then mark the width of the rings, adding ⅛ in. on each side of the bowl walls to be sure to have enough wood if the bowl should be a little off center when mounted on the lathe.

In this case, there are five rings plus a bottom. The rings are 1 in. thick. The bottom is made of three layers of wood with the grain of the center piece going 90° to that of the outside pieces. Although I have said that wood should not be stacked this way, it is okay here because the layers are thin, and better than having a solid-wood bottom. The grain in the rings runs around the circumference, so the wood will move up and down, but the circumference will not change. A piece of solid wood on the bottom would shrink and eventually break. As it is, the last layer of the bowl bottom will probably get small checks.

Now construct a drawing such as drawing **2**. In this bowl, each ring is made up of eight pieces. First, draw a straight line on your paper and then a line perpendicular to it. From the point where the two lines cross, the center, draw lines at 45° to divide the four quarters into eighths.

Now, set your dividers exactly the length of A from drawing **1** and draw an arc on drawing **2** as shown. Then set the dividers the length of B and draw another arc. Draw a straight line B1 and then, parallel to it and just touching the outside arc, draw line B2. Continue until you have drawn the length and width of all eight pieces for the five layers.

After drawing **2** is finished, cut the pieces of the rings to width and roughly cut the lengths to angle. Drawing **3** shows a way to cut the wood without waste, flipping the wood after each cut. Then set the miter gauge, taking the angle from the drawing. With eight pieces, the angle of each is 67½°. (Because you are working with a circle, all the pieces have the same angle, only the lengths of the pieces are different.)

After setting the miter gauge, cut the angle on eight pieces of scrap wood that are the same width and length. If the miter is off a fraction of a hair, it won't show up if you just check two pieces. If the angle is not correct, reset the miter gauge and try again. With the miter gauge set to the exact angle, you are ready to cut the pieces.

First, cut an end off each piece. Then for each ring put a stop on the miter gauge and cut the eight pieces to the exact length in the drawing **(4)**. Notice that the corner of the stop against the fence has been cut off, so no debris will be trapped there. An accumulation of sawdust and dirt would cause an inaccurate cut.

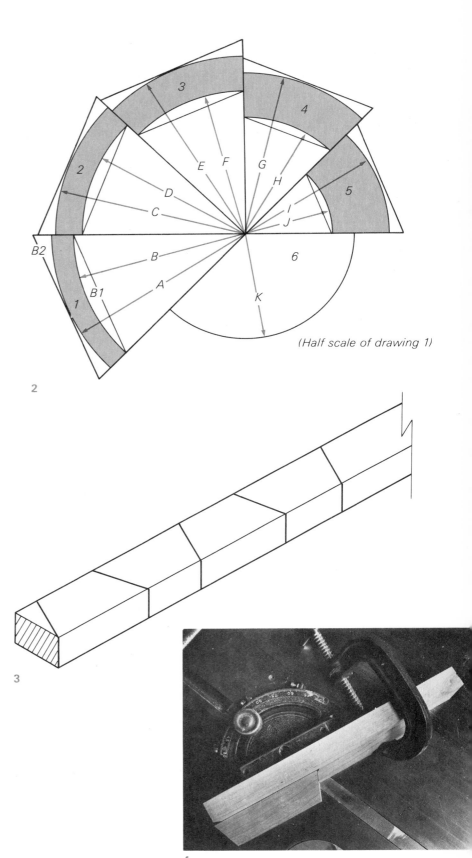

(Half scale of drawing 1)

2

3

4

5

6

When all the pieces are cut, glue them together in pairs with hot glue **(5,6)**, even if you're making a bowl that will have to be washed. Later on you can use a water-resistant glue such as Cascamite to put the rings together, and the joints glued with hot glue will be sandwiched in between the rings. Make sure to use glue on both ends and have paper underneath, so the wood won't stick to the bench. Rub the two pieces together to squeeze out the glue; after about a minute, the glue should be cold enough for you to let go. Set the pieces aside to cure.

When the pieces have been glued in pairs **(7)** and the glue has cured for about fifteen minutes, glue the pairs together **(8)**.

After about two hours, check to see if the two halves fit together **(9)**. If they don't, making them fit is not too difficult, but you'll need to make a jig for the table saw **(10)**.

To do this, cut out a piece of wood with sides that are exactly parallel and draw a line through the center. Put the center joint of one of the halves right on the line, and then check that distances A and B are exactly the same. Trace the piece to be cut on the jig and bandsaw out the jig carefully. After cutting on the table saw, distances C and D will be the same.

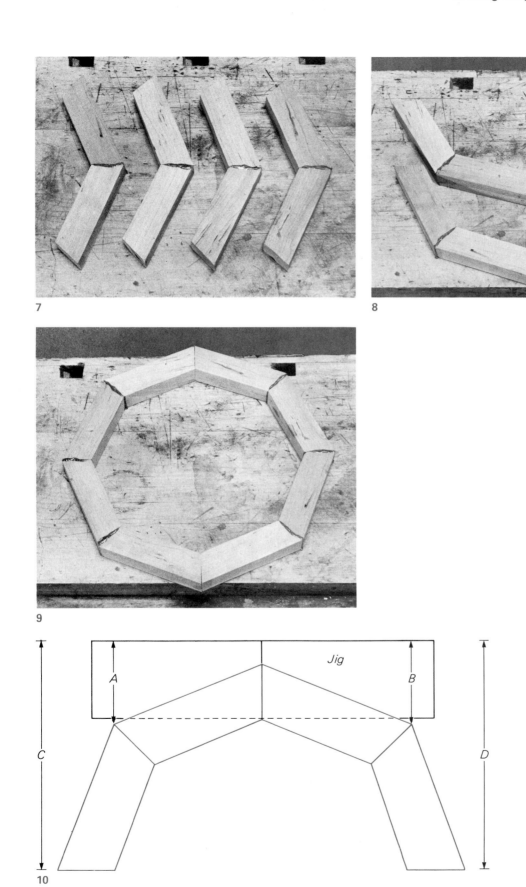

7

8

9

10

11

12

13

Set the fence so the blade just touches the joint **(11)**. Cutting too much off will make the circle into an oval.

Pull the jig away from the blade, then start the saw and make the cut **(12)**. Continue pushing the jig through and cut the other end **(13)**. Cut the other half the same way. The joint comes out perfectly. Now put the halves together using hot glue.

When you've assembled all the rings, let the glue cure about ten hours. Then clean the excess from both sides with a smoothing plane. You could also use a 6-in. belt sander for this, but that takes more skill and guts.

Before building up the bowl, find the center of each section of each of the rings and mark it. Square it across with a pencil **(14,15)**. Then stack the two lowest rings, alternating the alignment of marked centerlines and glue joints **(16)**.

When these rings are in position, mark the inside of the lowest ring for three or four brads **(17)**. The brads prevent the rings from slipping when they are being glued together. Don't put them in too deep. Because there is the extra ⅛ in. left on each side of the bowl walls, the brad marks will be removed when the bowl is turned.

Mark the next ring and proceed that way until the bowl is built up **(18)**.

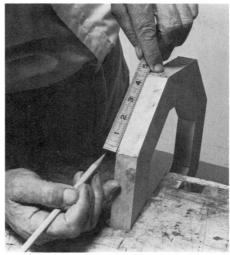

14   15

16

17

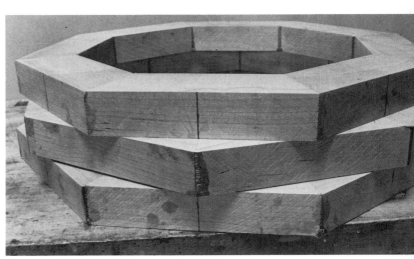

18

19

To center the bottom of the bowl, cut a piece of scrap wood to fit snugly inside the last ring. Find its center by measuring from one inside edge of the ring to the other **(19)**. Then do the same thing, turning the ruler 90°

Now set a compass to the radius of the bottom of the bowl **(20)**, and draw out the circle on the last ring **(21)**. Here again, use brads to prevent the bottom from slipping.

20

21

Next, mark out a scrap plate for the faceplate. The scrap plate should be ½ in. larger than the radius of the faceplate. Measure the diameter of the faceplate **(22)**, mark it on the scrap plate **(23)** and bandsaw it out. Center the scrap plate on the bowl bottom **(24)**.

With everything in place and marked, you're ready to glue the assembly together **(25)**. You can do this in one step but I prefer to glue up the rings first, and then the bottom and scrap plate. Beginners should glue two rings at a time.

Glue the scrap plate directly to the bowl without brown paper between. Because of the sharp corners and the danger of chattering, it's too dangerous to do otherwise. Remember to remove the brads before you start turning, and be careful not to turn through the first layer of the bottom of the bowl, because then you will be able to see the glueline and it looks awful.

When the bowl is finished, cut the plate off using a handsaw and sand the bottom. In this photo **(26)** the bowl is finished and oiled.

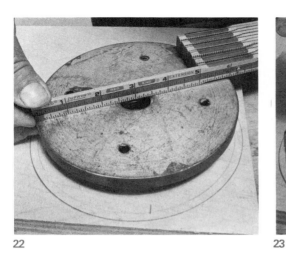

22

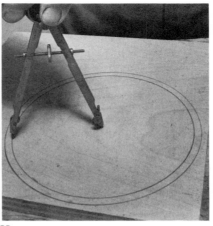

23

24

25

26

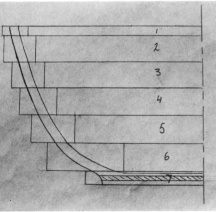

27

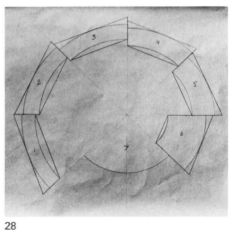

28

The way that I have shown for bricklaying a bowl is the fastest way. It is also a safe way, if you know what you are doing. Now I will tell you another way. This takes a bit more time but is safer, especially for a beginning turner. In this method, the rings of the bowl are bandsawn out and then glued on top of each other.

You'll still need to make full-scale drawings first **(27,28)**. Cut and glue the pieces together as before, into half sections, but don't glue the halves together until after bandsawing.

Here's a good way to mark the circles exactly. Glue a piece of wood in the center of a piece of cardboard — make the wood the same thickness as the rings so that a compass can rest on it **(29)**. From the drawing, take all the outside radii of the rings and draw the circumferences on the cardboard **(30)**. Then place each pair of halves on the cardboard so they fit inside the circumference of a particular ring **(31)**.

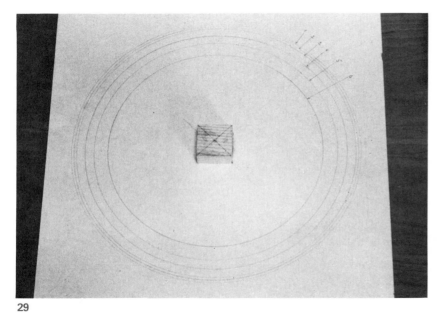

29

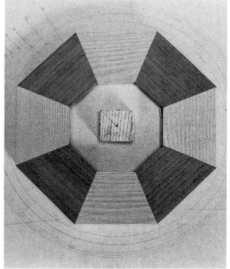

31

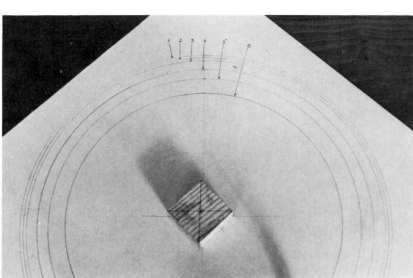

30

From your drawing, take the outside and inside radii **(32,33)** and transfer them to each ring with a compass. Because the halves are not glued together yet, it's best to have an extra pair of hands when doing this **(34)**.

Bandsaw the halves to the desired curve and then glue them together **(35)**. When the glue is dry, plane or sand the rings so that they are flat. This particular ring is the last one before the bottom.

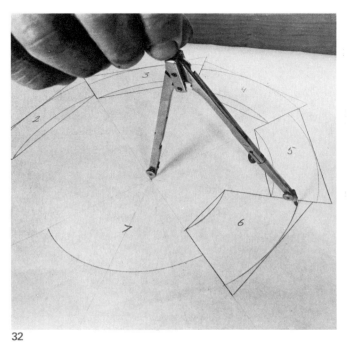

32

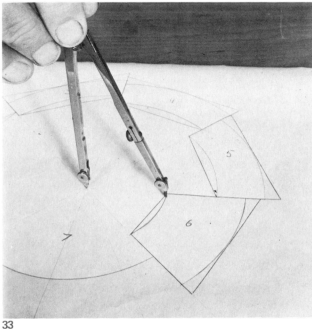

33

34

35

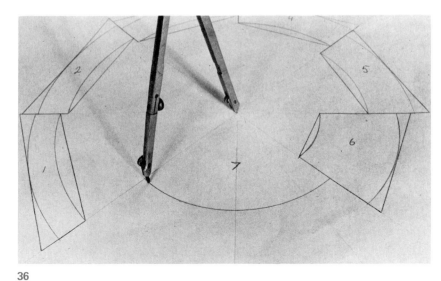

36

Now take the radius of the bottom of the bowl from the drawing **(36)**. In this case, the bottom of the bowl, which is laminated from three layers of walnut, measures 6 in., the same as the diameter of the faceplate. Because the scrap stock is already glued to the bottom stock here, just mark the bottom **(37)** and bandsaw it out.

Leaving the compass at the radius of the bowl bottom, put the last ring back on the cardboard and mark it for the bottom **(38)**.

Now stack the rings. Use a ruler to check the overhang and ensure that each ring is placed correctly **(39)**, or you might put each ring back on the cardboard and mark out the next ring on it before stacking.

37

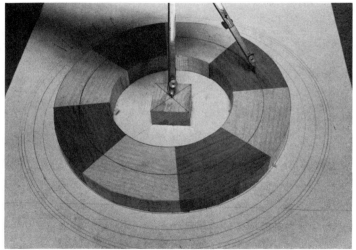

38

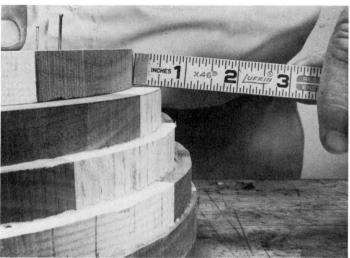

39

Also check that the joints on alternating rings line up **(40)**. Then mark the rings for the brads **(41)** — each should have four. Glue up everything, including the bottom and scrap plate **(42)**, with water-resistant glue.

When the glue has dried, screw on the faceplate **(43)** and turn the bowl. Make sure not to turn through the first layer of the bowl bottom. If you do, you'll reveal the glueline. Here **(44)** I went through on purpose and you can see the ugly blotch that results.

41

40

42

43

44

45

A bricklaid bowl has no end grain, so before sanding the outside, use a scraper blade (it's much faster) instead of a coarse grade of sandpaper **(45)**. Use a gooseneck scraper for the inside **(46)**.

In this bowl I used ash and walnut to empha- size the bricklaying **(47)**. When using differ- ent woods, be sure to pick woods of similar density so that they will move together. For example, if the walnut in this bowl were ebony, which does not shrink much, there would be conflict between its rate of shrinkage and that of the ash, and the bowl would eventually fall apart. ☐

46

47

Plywood and Veneer
Chapter 6

History

The art of veneering has had a checkered career. It was practiced in Egypt 3500 years ago, as well as in ancient Greece and Rome. During the Middle Ages, there seems to have been less veneering in furniture construction; but veneering made a comeback in Italy during the fifteenth century, and the art spread through Europe, reaching a climax in skill and artistry in eighteenth-century Germany, France and England. Interest in the art of veneering declined again, however, in the nineteenth century, with the introduction of production machinery.

Throughout history, the lack of glues resistant to water and heat has been the biggest problem in veneering. Today there is a resurgence of interest in veneering, which, I think, is largely due to modern adhesives and the development of plywood.

Many people talk about plywood as "that modern glued-up stuff," but this is ridiculous when you consider that the basis of plywood construction is the age-old process of veneering. Because plywood makes an excellent ground surface on which to veneer, craftsmen should at least know how it is made and used, so I'll talk about that first. ☐

Plywood

Plywood is made by gluing together several thin layers of wood with alternating grains. It has distinct advantages and disadvantages, so there is usually little doubt about where and when to use it instead of solid wood.

Its biggest advantage is that it is more stable and won't change dimension, except in thickness. The crossply construction in veneer-core plywood gives about 50% long-grain to long-grain gluing surface, allowing the use of less complicated joints in some applications. There is also less waste for the craftsman, because there are no knots, checks or other defects that must be cut out. Plywood is also economical to manufacture, since almost all of a tree can be used, and it is often more economical to work than solid wood because it's ready to be cut up and joined. Solid wood has to be edge-joined, thickness-planed, and so forth, before joints can be made.

The greatest disadvantage of plywood is that it is more difficult to repair than solid wood. This is because the veneers are so thin. Also, the joints usually have to be hidden and the edges faced. Besides that, plywood cannot be shaped or carved. Along the grain, solid wood is much stronger than plywood, while across the grain, veneer-core plywood is stronger.

The first fumbling efforts to use plywood in the mass production of furniture were in the 1920s, and since then plywood has become indispensable. The flush corners and edges of modern furniture and the development of frame-and-panel construction into plain, unbroken surfaces would have been impossible without the dimensional stability of plywood. Even architecture has been revolutionized by the availability of standard-size sheets of wood that are stronger than ordinary lumber. ☐

Plywood Manufacture

Veneers for plywood are cut in one of four ways, depending on the species of the lumber and the use to which the veneer will be put. I will describe these methods briefly before getting into plywood construction to give an idea of how veneer is prepared.

Most veneer is rotary cut **(1)**. This method requires first removing the bark and steaming the log. Then the log is placed between centers on a large veneer lathe and revolved into a knife. As the log turns, the knife automatically advances into the stock at a controlled rate, which determines the thickness of the veneer.

Rotary-cut veneer doesn't have the fine figure of sliced veneer, because when it is cut the veneer is peeled off the log like a sheet of paper toweling pulled from a roll. Because the cuts are always parallel to the annual rings, the grain of the veneer looks unnaturally stretched and doesn't have much character. This mahogany **(2)** has been rotary cut. Some of the color of the wood is also destroyed during steaming. Rotary-cut veneer is used mostly for core stock in hardwood plywood, for crossbanding and as facing on cheap plywood.

For face veneer, the finest hardwood logs are used and the veneer is usually sliced instead of rotary cut. Here again, the log is steamed first. There are several ways to slice veneer. Most often the log will be pushed into a fixed knife and then automatically advanced between cuts so each slice is the exact same thickness, usually $\frac{1}{28}$ in. The pieces are kept in order as they come from the machine so they can be matched. Sliced veneers are sold in flitches, bundles containing all the stock from one log or from one section of a large log. This makes it possible to panel a whole room with face veneer from the same tree and to match the grain from one veneer leaf to the next.

Half-round veneer is similar to sliced veneer, but it is cut on the veneer lathe. The log and the staylog to which it's bolted in eccentric chunks are mounted on the lathe. As the staylog revolves, it presents only a small part of a large circle to be sliced into veneer. Veneer cut this way has interesting figure.

The fourth and oldest method of producing veneer is by bandsawing with a thin blade, which makes a narrow kerf. Even so, as much wood is wasted as is saved. Because this method produces so much waste, it is not often used commercially. It's still the best way, however, for a woodworker to make his or her own veneer.

All veneer must be dried carefully after cutting. In drying, the veneer passes between rollers and heated platters that are arranged to keep the veneer as flat as possible.   □

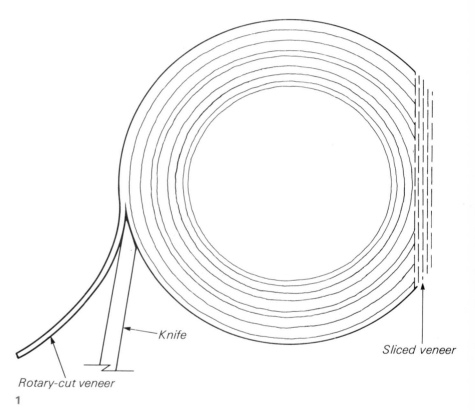

Knife

Sliced veneer

Rotary-cut veneer

1

2

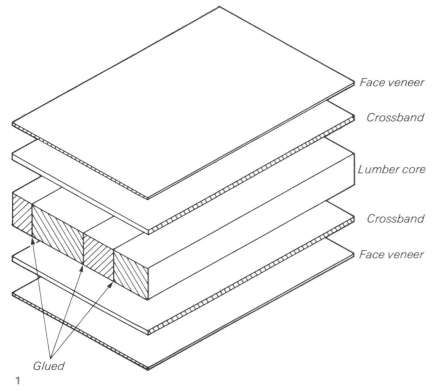

Face veneer

Crossband

Lumber core

Crossband

Face veneer

Glued

1

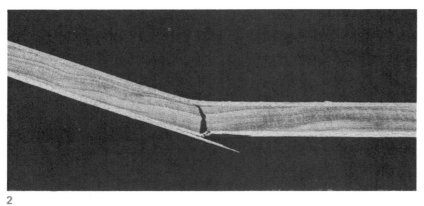

2

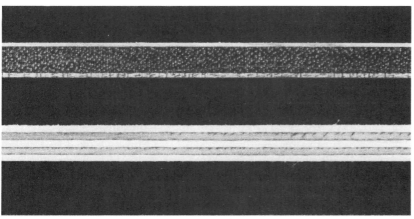

3

Plywood Construction

Plywood is always glued up of an uneven number of plies of various thicknesses, depending on the final thickness of the sheet itself **(1)**. But whatever the thickness, the grain direction of any ply must run at right angles to that of the adjacent plies. This crossing of the grains gives plywood its uniform strength and dimensional stability.

In Europe during the 1930s, synthetic resin glue was developed. This glue provides a strong bond and has a great resistance to moisture. Today plywood is usually glued with a synthetic resin glue.

The two outside veneers on a piece of plywood are called the face veneers and are usually 1/28 in. thick. The layers under the face veneers are called crossbands and in good plywood are usually thicker than the faces. The wood between crossbands, which constitutes the center, is called the core. Plywood is available with either a veneer core or a lumber core.

Veneer-core plywood is the best known, most popular plywood. The thinner the veneer used to build up the core, the greater the strength of the plywood. I would never use, for example, three-ply 1/4-in. plywood. In most cases such plywood is made of cheap materials, especially in the core, so any imperfection telegraphs right through the face veneers **(2)**. Assuming that the face veneers are 1/28 in. thick, the core will be about 1/5 in. thick, and because the grain of the core crosses the grain of the faces, the plywood is weak and breaks easily. If 1/4-in. plywood is made with five plies, the center ply and the face veneers will run in the same direction, making the plywood stronger and more stable. This photo **(3)** shows both types of 1/4-in. plywood.

The quality of veneer-core plywood varies greatly. This **(4)** is the cheapest type, where anything goes in as long as it is wood. It's full of cracks and voids. Voids make the face veneers weak in those places because there is nothing to back them up.

Baltic birch plywood, made in Russia, is a better veneer-core plywood **(5)**. When it was first imported the Russians and Americans were not on friendly terms; so rather than call it Russian plywood, the Americans named it after the Baltic sea, to which the Russians have access. On the west coast of the United States, Baltic birch plywood is called Russian plywood. In some areas it is also called Finnish plywood.

Baltic birch plywood is made to metric dimensions: Standard sheets are 150 cm. by 150 cm. (roughly 5 ft. by 5 ft.). It is birch the whole way through and has no knotholes. Its edges, which are very clean, can be exposed. The plies are very thin — a ¼-in. thick piece of Baltic birch plywood will have five plies. Disadvantages are that it twists if not held down and lately I have found that sometimes the plies separate.

Another good veneer-core plywood is made in the Philippines and sold under the commercial name lauan. It is very stable and has a good core, free of knotholes **(6)**. The core veneer is thicker than that of Baltic birch, but because lauan moves very little, this is fine. A piece of ¾-in. plywood will have seven plies, including the face veneers. Lauan is close in color to mahogany. A similar product made out of shina (another commercial name for limewood) is much lighter in color.

Lumber-core plywood is made up of two face veneers, two crossbands and a solid-wood core. Because the core is considerably thicker than the crossbands and has grain running in the same direction as the face veneers', it has great strength lengthwise.

The core of most American commercial lumber-core plywood is made up of edge-joined strips, commonly of poplar or basswood, although mahogany is better. These strips vary in width, but 3 in. is usually the maximum. They are glued together and dressed to the necessary thickness, and then the crossbands and face veneers are glued on. Lumber-core plywood can twist because the glued-up core acts like one piece of wood.

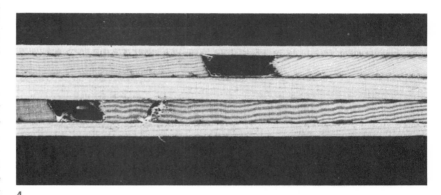

4

5

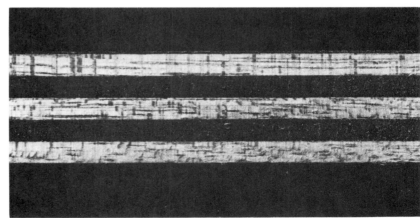

6

Imported lauan plywood is also available in lumber core. The difference between the lauan lumber core and the ordinary commercial kind is that the core strips in the lauan are not glued up into one solid sheet. They're held together by the crossband plies, with small spaces between the strips **(7)**. This allows each strip to move independently, making the plywood more stable and more suitable for cabinetmaking.

When I was an apprentice in Denmark, most lumber-core stock was constructed without face veneers and craftsmen put on their own. Now this unfaced lumber core is available in the United States, in 8x4 sheets. Unfaced veneer-core plywood is also available in the same-size sheets. Both are called platform stock and come in lauan and shina.

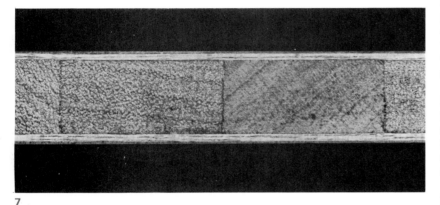

7

Beware of plywood having face veneers of different woods because, with plywood, the cardinal rule is that what is done to one side must be done to the other. If walnut is on the front face and poplar is on the back, for example, the woods will expand and contract differently and cause the whole sheet to twist. Sometimes it is okay to use plywood that is faced with different species, as when making panel walls or drawer bottoms. In these applications, the backs won't be seen and the plywood will be locked in place, unable to move. Plywood having the same species of face veneer front and back is available, although usually the quality of the front face is better and has fewer defects.

Because most plywood is made for builders, not cabinetmakers, manufacturers sometimes try to cut costs by using a core of fir. Never veneer directly over fir plywood or buy plywood where the face veneers are bound directly to fir — the grain of the fir will eventually telegraph through because of the difference between the wood's spring and summer growth.

I think it is always worthwhile to buy the highest-quality plywood possible. For a craftsman to try to save a few dollars on material doesn't make sense when you consider all the hours invested in making a piece of furniture.

Plywood grading The U.S. Department of Commerce has established voluntary standards for grading hardwood plywood. This grading system is different from the one used to grade softwood plywood. Premium-grade veneers are given the symbol *A*, while other-quality veneers are designated by a number: good grade, *1*, sound grade, *2*; utility grade, *3*; backing grade, *4*. There is also a specialty grade, *SP*. Any combination is possible, the first symbol representing the quality of the face veneer and the second the quality of the back veneer. Plywood grade *A-3*, for example, has a premium-quality face veneer and a utility-grade back veneer. The best would be *A-A*.

When ordering hardwood plywood, always give the dimensions in the order of thickness, width and length. This way, you'll be sure the grain on the face veneer will run along the length. □

Other Materials

There are other materials that can be veneered or that come already faced with veneer. These are sold under the commercial names of particleboard and fiberboard. There are both advantages and disadvantages to using them.

The greatest advantage is that veneer can be applied to them with its grain going in any direction, because particleboard and fiberboard have no grain direction of their own. These materials are also less expensive than plywood. A disadvantage, however, is that they are not nearly as strong, and they're not easy to join together, either, because the joints must be reinforced with splines made out of some other material.

Particleboard is made out of wood flakes, chips or sawdust coated with glue and pressed into sheets. Consequently, its edges are not very attractive (1) and usually a facing must be glued on. The surface of particleboard also is not very smooth (2) and is not good for painting.

Fiberboard is made out of wood fibers coated with glue and pressed into sheets. It has edges that are very smooth (3), and they stay that way even after being shaped (4). The surface (5) is smooth enough for painting, but a drawback to using fiberboard is that it is quite heavy.

The major disadvantage of particleboard and fiberboard is that they will bow if used to make doors that slide in a track on the bottom. This is because there is no grain direction to support the weight. If you are making doors more than 3 ft. tall, either put a wide solid-wood facing on both edges of the doors or hang them from a frame on the top, so they won't warp.

If you are making doors that hang, put a solid-wood facing on both sides for the hinge screws. Do this also if making tall cabinets. Get a shelf or stretcher going across every 2 ft. or 3 ft. or else use a wide facing in the front or the back. If the back is screwed on, a wide facing might not be necessary there.

When screwing into particleboard or fiberboard, I always put glue on the screw thread to give it more strength or I glue in dowels for the screw to penetrate. Here (6) a hinge is inserted right into the particleboard without a facing. The screws will go through the dowels and hold the hinge securely. This makes a nice detail, but if you choose to paint the door, the dowels won't show.   □

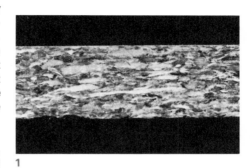

1

2

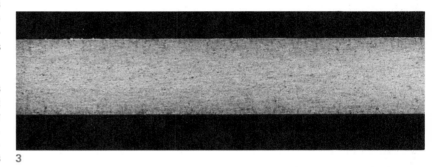

3

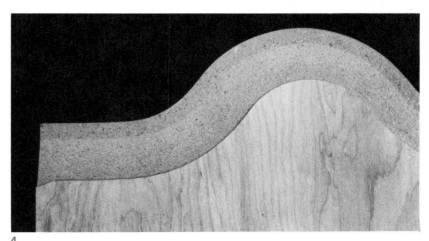

4

5

6

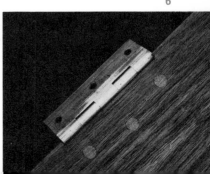

1

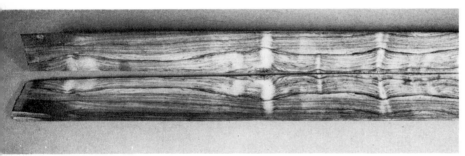

2

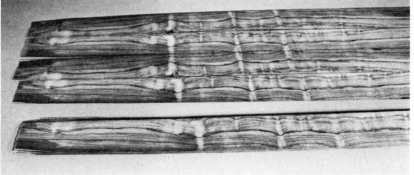

3

4

Veneering

If you are building a veneered cabinet where the veneer has to match the whole way around and from top to bottom, you will usually have to do your own veneering. Here are four rules to follow:

First, always take the pieces of veneer from the top or the bottom of a flitch **(1)**. If you pull out some sheets from the center, the grain can no longer be matched perfectly and the flitch will lose its value. This is the reason you pay twice as much for small quantities of veneer as for a whole flitch.

There are two ways to match veneer on a panel. One is called bookmatching, because the first two pieces of veneer are opened like a book **(2)**. Then the next two are opened the same way and the four pieces are put together **(3)**. This is usually how good-quality sheets of hardwood plywood are faced. The other way of matching is to use veneers in the order they come off the flitch without flipping them **(4)**. This is called slipmatching.

Trees for face veneer are hard to find and very valuable. If you have a nice walnut, cherry, oak or any other hardwood tree, don't cut it down for firewood, because it might be worth a great deal of money.

The second rule in veneering is that you should never use veneer thicker than $\frac{1}{28}$ in.; veneer that is too thick will definitely crack. For example, assume that the face veneer in the drawing **(5)** is $\frac{1}{4}$ in. thick and 48 in. wide. The glue will hold the bottom of the veneer at 48 in., but the top of the veneer will shrink as it dries. The edges will bend in at first, but after that, the veneer will start to crack.

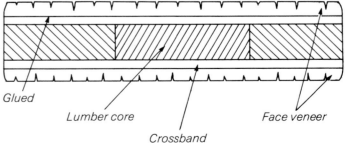
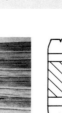

Glued

Lumber core

Crossband

Face veneer

5

Third, always cross the grain direction of the face veneers and the crossbands **(6,7)**. The angle doesn't have to be 90°, but it should be no smaller than 15°. If you place the grain of the face veneer parallel to the crossband's, the veneer will crack later on.

If the grain of the face veneer has to run in different directions **(8)**, either the plywood has to be cut so the grain is angled at 45° or some inexpensive veneer has to be applied to both sides as crossbanding that runs at an angle of 45°. Particleboard or fiberboard, neither of which has any grain direction, could also be used.

This rule changes, however, when applying face veneer to solid wood, where the grain of the wood and of the veneer should run in the same direction so the two layers of wood can move together as a unit. You can also use thicker veneer on solid wood.

The fourth rule of veneering is that you must always do the same thing to both sides of the ground surface. If you don't, the piece will definitely bow and twist.

This piece was veneered only on one side and the pictures **(9,10)** show what happened. The veneer absorbed the moisture from the glue and expanded before it was clamped down. When the piece came out of the press, the veneer started to dry and shrink, twisting the plywood.

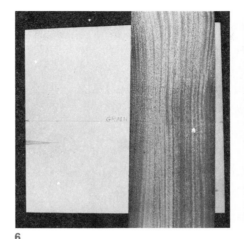

6

7

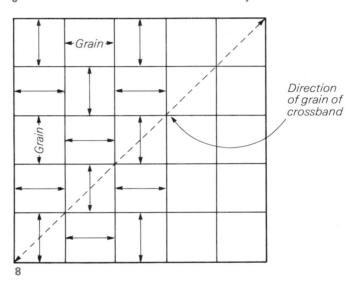

8

9

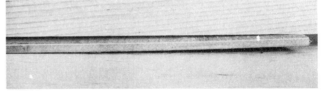

10

11

12

13

14

Knowing that veneer will shrink when drying, I started to experiment to see if I could take advantage of that to make tubes without a form. I was lucky and it worked. Here's how it happened.

I took two pieces of mahogany and one of rosewood. The grain of the mahogany was 90° to the grain of the rosewood (**11**).

The mahogany veneer measured 19¹¹⁄₁₆ in. in width when it was dry (**12**). I soaked it in water for a minute or two. Then I placed it between two boards with five layers of newspaper on each side to absorb some of the water, but I did not put pressure on. After ten to fifteen minutes, I removed the boards. The mahogany measured 20⅜ in. — it had expanded ¹¹⁄₁₆ in. (**13**).

For gluing I used Cascamite mixed very thick because the mahogany veneer was already moist. If the glue had been mixed to the regular consistency, it would have been too thin for this job and the pieces would not have stuck together.

I glued the wet mahogany to the dry rosewood and placed the piece between two boards with six pieces of newspaper on each side (**14**). I left it for about six hours; the time depends on the room temperature.

The minute I took it out of the press, the piece started to roll up, so I had to hurry to scrape and sand it while it was still relatively flat **(15)**. Then I placed the ends of the piece on two boards so that the veneer would be pulled down by its own weight and would dry faster **(16)**.

I rolled up the piece **(17)** when it was fairly dry. (Don't let the glue dry completely or the piece might break.) I overlapped the ends and clamped them between two boards **(18)**. After drying there was no springback **(19)**. □

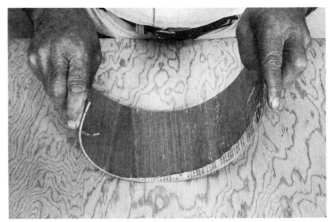

15

16

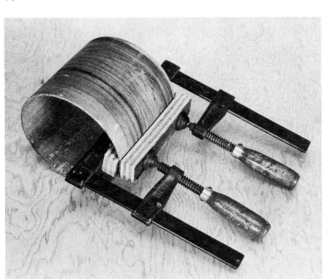

17

18

19

Glues and Gluing

I use three kinds of glue for veneering, depending on the job. They are hot glue, Titebond and Cascamite. The glue you use is as important as the way you use it. I would never use a new glue on a piece without testing it for a couple of years first. It is very important to test new glues on a regular basis because there are so many different ones on the market today, all claiming that they can glue everything but broken hearts. Each craftsman has a favorite, and if it works, that's fine. To me the most important thing about a glue is how it holds over the years.

This is the main reason I like hot glue. It goes way back to the Egyptians, so you know you can rely on it. Hot glue is made from animal hides, blood and bones. It is made liquid with water and heat. I use hot glue for hammer-veneering (p. 126) and anywhere I can apply heat to the work after it is clamped up, such as when using sandbags (p. 156). The advantage of hot glue in this case is that the veneer doesn't get a chance to absorb moisture and expand. This is because the glue is applied to the ground stock and allowed to cool before the veneer is applied. The veneer is then clamped up and the glue remelted. I also use hot glue for vacuum-forming. Another of its advantages is that the work can be taken out of the press after a couple of hours when the glue is cold. But hot glue is not suited for use in warm and humid climates.

Hot glue is melted in a glue pot, which is like a double boiler. When buying a glue pot, get one that will hold water between the glue container and the outer container. Because water constantly evaporates from the glue, hot water has to be added frequently to maintain the glue's consistency, and it's nice to have some right in the pot. Also, in hammer-veneering, after the veneer is glued down and has to be trimmed, the veneer saw has to be submerged in hot water so it will be warm and wet. If you can't get your water from the glue pot, you have to keep an extra container with hot water nearby.

Judging whether your glue is the proper consistency is something you have to learn to do through experience, but if the glue drops from the brush like honey it is probably right. You will know the glue is spoiled if it stays liquid after it is cooled.

To check that the glue is made correctly and is ready to use, put a drop between your fingers and rub them together, applying pressure. You should be able to squeeze out all the excess easily after about a minute. If the room is around average temperature, about 60° to 70° F, your fingers should start to stick together as the hot glue gets cold and starts to bond. The glue won't reach full strength, however, until it has dried completely, which takes about 24 hours.

Titebond is an aliphatic resin glue. It is a good strong glue, water and heat-resistant, with a short setup time. I use this glue when I'm not gluing up too many pieces and have enough time to get everything in the press before the glue dries. Titebond doesn't have to be mixed or heated so it's always ready to be used, and it has a long shelf life. Brushes and rollers used with it are fairly easy to clean with water.

Cascamite is a plastic-resin glue that comes in powder form and has to be mixed with water. When you use Cascamite, be sure to stir the powder well before adding the water, to avoid lumps. Because of its long setup time, Cascamite is the glue most often used for veneering. I use it when I have many pieces to veneer or when a piece is large and takes a long time to glue up.

Cascamite is water and heat-resistant but has a short pot life, remaining usable after it is mixed for only a few hours. Don't buy large cans of this glue unless you intend to use it up quickly, because each time you open the can you allow moisture to get in. After a while, the powder in the bottom of the can won't be any good.

Unless you become an expert at opening and closing the can without admitting moisture and learn to mix up only the amount you need, Cascamite can be very expensive to use. Some people put flour in Cascamite to stretch it, but I don't like to risk weakening it. This glue is easy to clean off brushes and rollers, however, so you can save some money there by using them over and over again. With some other resin glues, brushes and rollers can be used only once or twice.

One thing to keep in mind when using Cascamite is that it shrinks as it dries. Here **(1)** the can it is mixed in is 2½ in. in diameter. The glue shrank ³⁄₁₆ in. in diameter and the same in height. If glue is trapped under veneer, the veneer will eventually crack. Also, if there is an imperfection in the surface that is full of glue, the glue will pull the veneer down into the hole after a while.

When applying any glue, be sure there is enough on the work and that it is evenly spread. Don't put so much on that it runs all over the work and the bench. Just put on enough so that a little will be squeezed out along the edges. A good way to spread Titebond or Cascamite is with a paint roller, but always put a little extra along the edges to make sure that they will be glued down.

Apply glue only to the surface of the piece to be veneered, never directly to the veneer. This rule pertains to all veneering but hammer-veneering. If you put glue on the veneer **(2)**, one side will expand and the whole piece will roll up like a scroll **(3)** before you can get it into the press.

Never use contact cement for veneering. I've seen it fail too many times and it is just about impossible to repair.   □

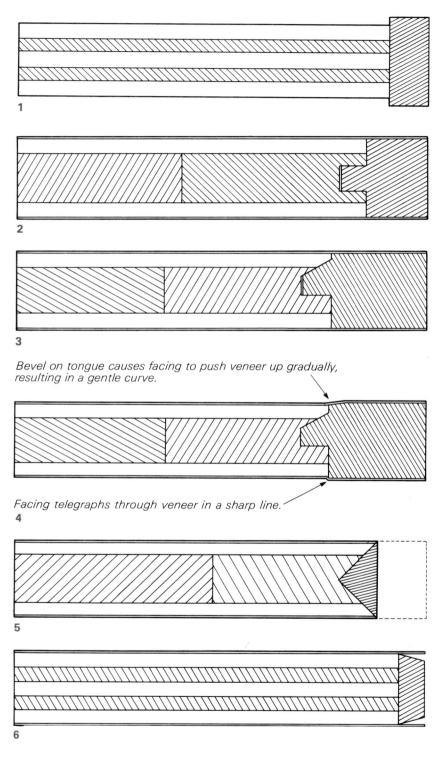

Bevel on tongue causes facing to push veneer up gradually, resulting in a gentle curve.

Facing telegraphs through veneer in a sharp line.

Facings

When using plywood for furniture, you ordinarily have to apply a facing or a piece of veneer to cover up the plywood edges. Of course, if you use Baltic birch, the edges are attractive and can be exposed.

There are several ways to apply facings. They are usually glued on before the face veneer is applied, but you can do it afterward, too — the methods are the same. The exception to this is the beveled tongue-and-groove joint, which should be used only before the face veneer is applied. Whichever method you choose, the facing should be ⅛ in. wider than the thickness of the plywood so it can be planed flush with the surface later.

The simplest way to apply a facing is to glue a ¼-in. piece of wood directly to the edge of the plywood without any joint **(1)**.

Facings ½ in. to 1 in. thick should be applied using a tongue-and-groove joint **(2)**.

Where a facing is 1 in. thick or over and goes across the grain of the veneer, a beveled tongue-and-groove joint should be used **(3)**. If you were to use a regular tongue and groove, the differences in movement between the plywood and the facing would cause the facing to telegraph right through the veneer, especially across the grain, revealing a sharp line. This would not be as noticeable lengthwise. With a beveled tongue, the differences between the two pieces are minimized because the facing pushes the veneer up gradually. Instead of a sharp line, you get a gentle curve **(4)**. The same is the case if the facing shrinks.

If the face veneer is already on and you don't want the facing to show, a good way to apply it is with a *V*-groove **(5)**. This is also a good way to apply facings over 1 in. thick.

After applying the facing of your choice, the next step is making it flush with the surface, using a plane, belt sander or router. Be careful not to round over the facing, because this will keep the edge of the veneer from being glued properly **(6)**.

The fastest, easiest way to get a facing flush is with a router. Screw a piece of wood to one side of the router base and set a flat-bottomed bit flush with its bottom **(7)**. Push the piece of wood down on the work and move the router forward **(8)**. If the facing is thick, trim it in several passes.

Sand lightly after routing **(9)** to be sure the facing doesn't protrude above the surface, being careful not to round over the edge.

When gluing facings on all four edges of a piece of plywood, first fit all the facings without glue. Then remove two of the facings and apply glue to them, leaving the other two to guide the ones being glued **(10)**. As soon as they're clamped in place **(11)**, remove the guide facings so they don't get stuck. Remember to put strips of wood between the facings and the clamps to keep the clamps from marring the work. When the glue is dry, plane the facings flush and then glue on the next two, trimming the edges flush as before.

Now you're ready to apply the veneer. If there are any imperfections in the plywood, such as dents, cracks or holes, fill them with powdered chalk (whiting) mixed with thin hot glue. The mixture should be like putty, so use just enough glue to keep the whiting together. Fill the cracks so that the filler is above the surface. This way, when the filler dries, it can be sanded flush with the surface. If you use too much glue, or plaster of paris instead of whiting, the filler will be harder than the wood and won't sand flush. If properly mixed, the filler will be porous enough to absorb the glue that is applied for the veneer. ☐

7

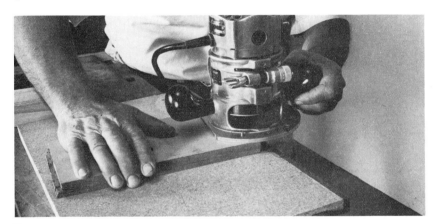

8

9

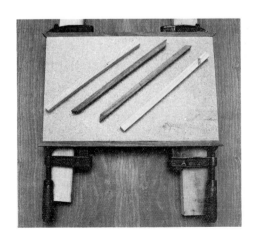

10

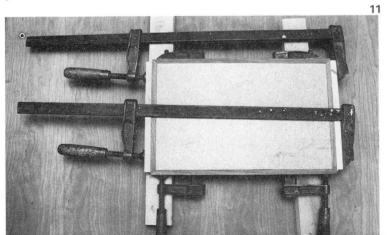

11

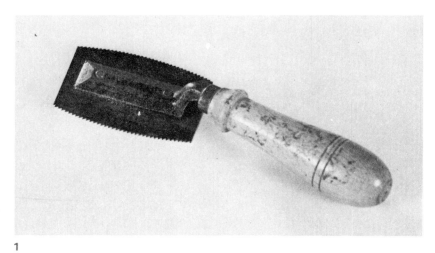

1

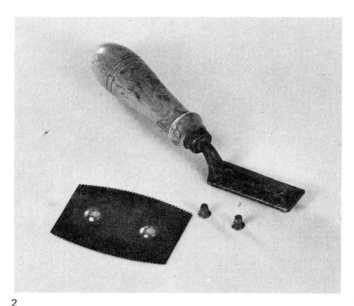

2

3

Hammer-Veneering

Hammer-veneering is the old way of applying veneer to solid wood or to plywood. Hammer-veneering can be done very quickly, but its biggest advantage is that you don't need a veneer press, cauls or clamps. In the method of veneering common today, the size of the work is limited by the size of the veneer press or of the clamps, but with hammer-veneering you could veneer the whole world if you wanted to.

The main tool for hammer-veneering is the veneer hammer, which is not used for hammering at all but for applying pressure. The hammer has a narrow face, so you can transmit the strength of your arm and the weight of your body to a tiny area of veneer. The veneer is held down by hot glue, which sticks as soon as it is cold. You spread the hot glue on the ground surface and the veneer, then use the hammer to squeeze out the glue before it cools off. You can resoften the glue as necessary with a warm iron. Hammer-veneering is usually the easiest way to fix furniture when there is broken veneer or an air bubble under the veneer.

The veneer saw   A veneer saw or knife is used to cut the veneer to size **(1)**. It is called both a saw and a knife because it is filed like a saw and sharpened like a knife to make a smooth cut for joining veneers. The curved blade of the saw is only about 3 in. long. The blade can be removed for sharpening and the handle is offset **(2)**, so when you're using the saw against a straightedge you won't scrape your hands.

Both edges of a veneer saw can be sharpened with a small triangular file **(3)**. I file each tooth at 60° to the surface of the blade with no back or front **(4)** so that I can use the saw in either direction. This makes for a slower but smoother cut.

After the teeth are filed sharp like a saw's, they are sharpened so that the cross section of each is like a knife's. Rotate the saw along each curve against a stone, holding the blade at a shallow angle but being careful not to lose the points of the teeth **(5)**.

When using the saw, keep a board under the veneer so you don't cut into the top of your bench. Use a straightedge to guide the saw as you cut **(6)**.

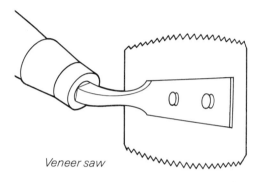

Veneer saw

4

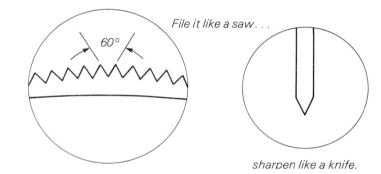

File it like a saw...

60°

sharpen like a knife.

5

6

7

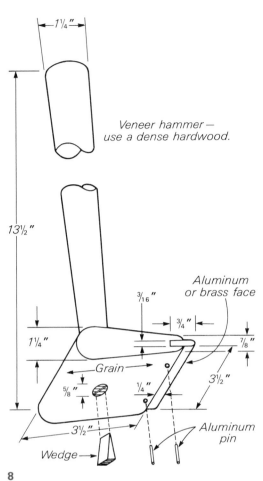

*Veneer hammer —
use a dense hardwood.*

1¼″

13½″

3/16″

*Aluminum
or brass face*

¾″

7/8″

1¼″

Grain

3½″

5/8″

¼″

3½″

Wedge

*Aluminum
pin*

8

Veneer hammers   Veneer hammers vary in design. Hammers made out of steel like this one **(7)** are available commercially. If you want to make your own, plan on having a long handle and use a hardwood wedge with an insert of aluminum or brass for the working edge **(8)**. The edge must be straight and about 3½ in. wide, with a round profile to squeeze out the glue from underneath the veneer. Follow the dimensions in the drawing and use a hard, heavy wood such as maple. Before using a new hammer, soak it in raw linseed oil so the glue won't stick to it, but let it dry before using.

Edge veneering   It is clumsy and time-consuming to veneer edges with clamps, but it is fast and easy with a veneer hammer. It doesn't matter whether the edge is straight or curved. Cut the strip of veneer to be applied about ⅛ in. wider than the thickness of the plywood. If you cut the veneer too wide, the excess sticking in the air will dry before the glue has cured and will curl away from the edges of the wood.

Wet the veneer on both sides to make it more flexible and also to see which way it naturally wants to arch. Glue it concave side down, so the arch will keep it in place **(9)**. If you do it the other way, you'll have trouble keeping the outer edges stuck down **(10)**.

9

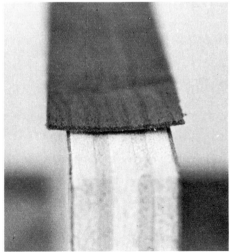

10

Begin by brushing glue onto the edge to be veneered **(11)**, then place the outside surface of the veneer right in the glue. Brush glue onto the other side of the veneer **(12)**. The glue that smears on the outside will help the hammer slide and prevent the outside of the veneer from drying too fast, which might pull up the edges. You can scrape the glue off the outside later.

Now flip the veneer over and hold it in place with one hand — hot glue is slippery. Hold the hammer in your other hand and press down hard to squeeze out the excess glue all along the edge **(13)**. You have to work fast to get all the veneer down while the glue is still hot. The minute the glue gets cold, the veneer will stick. Keep an old iron warmed up and handy, so if the veneer is not glued down right, you can remelt the glue before going back over it with the hammer. Don't have the iron so hot that the glue burns or you will regret it. Burned glue has an unpleasant smell that hangs around for a long time.

11

12

13

14

Use the veneer saw to clean off excess glue and trim the veneer while the glue is still soft. Remove the glue pot from the water jacket and dip the sawblade into the hot water **(14)** so it will be wet and warm and the glue won't stick to it. Then cut off the excess veneer at both ends, holding the work up at an angle **(15)**. Next, stand the work on edge, tilt it a little to apply pressure right at the corner to be cleaned and saw off the excess veneer **(16)**. Dip the blade in hot water after each cutting. After the work is trimmed, put the piece aside to dry for about 24 hours.

It doesn't make any difference if the edge is curved. You can veneer it exactly as if it were straight **(17)**. If the work isn't straight, however, you must wait until the glue is hard and dry to remove the excess veneer and squeezed-out glue and use a block plane or a smoothing plane to clean it off.

15

16

17

Veneering large surfaces   To veneer a large surface you will have to edge-join pieces of veneer, either lengthwise, across, or both. The edge joint must be very accurate. I overlap the two pieces of veneer about ½ in. at the joint, then cut through both pieces at the same time after they are glued down and lift out the waste.

Begin by figuring out how you want the veneer to match, and mark the location of each piece on the work **(18)**. The veneer should overhang the surface to be veneered by about ½ in. on all sides so you can trim the waste off later. Work on one section at a time. Moisten the veneer to see which way it wants to curl. Brush hot glue onto the ground surface **(19)**.

Place the veneer in the glue, concave side up, exactly as in edge veneering. Apply glue to the veneer **(20)**, then flip it over and position it. Use the veneer hammer to secure it somewhere in the center first **(21)**.

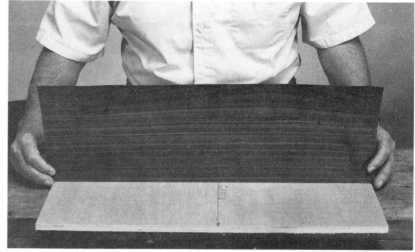

18

19

20

21

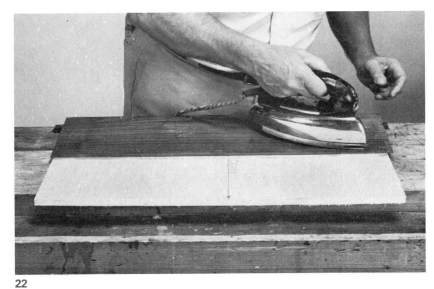

Now use a warm iron to melt the glue under a small section of the veneer **(22)**. Push down with the veneer hammer as hard as you can, using the weight of your body to squeeze out the excess glue **(23)**. Try to avoid going directly across the grain with the hammer, but do hold the hammer at an angle to the grain so that the glue will be squeezed out toward the edges. When that part is glued down, move to the next area and repeat, proceeding until the whole sheet is stuck tight.

Now apply glue to the next sheet of veneer and proceed in exactly the same way. Don't forget to overlap the edges to be joined ½ in. When both sheets are stuck, use a straight-edge and a sharp, warm, wet veneer saw to cut through both sheets at once **(24,25)**.

22

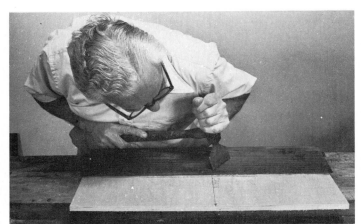

23

24

25

Remove the scrap veneer from the top **(26)**, carefully lift up the top sheet and pull out the scrap from underneath **(27)**. Butt the edges together, heat with the iron **(28)**, and push hard with the hammer to squeeze out all the excess glue through the line of the joint **(29)**. Here it is okay to use the hammer going across the grain because both pieces are already glued down.

26

27

28

29

30

31

When the joint is down tight, press a strip of heavy brown paper over it to prevent it from opening while drying **(30)**. After the glue is dry, use a sharp scraper blade or cabinet scraper to remove the paper and excess glue, but set a heavier burr than normal on the blade (chapter 2). A good seam should be invisible.

You must be sure that no air bubbles are under the veneer. If you can't see the bubbles when you push down with the hammer, tap the surface lightly with your finger and listen for hollow spots. If you don't glue down these hollow spots, they will eventually crack. The veneer I used for this demonstration was very curly in one spot in the center and would not stay down, so I covered it with brown paper and clamped on a warm block of wood to reheat the glue and hold the piece down tightly while the glue cooled and dried **(31)**. If you don't notice an air bubble until several days or months later, just use water, heat and pressure to work the piece down. The glue will still hold. If this doesn't work, another way is to cut the bubble with a razor blade or sharp knife, inject some glue underneath and then clamp down (p. 145). ☐

Hard-to-Handle Veneer

Some veneer can be brittle, wrinkled and hard to handle, such as this bird's-eye elm veneer **(1)**. It can be flattened by soaking in water and then pressing between two flat boards with two or three sheets of newspaper on each side of the veneer. The problem is that the water will cause the veneer to expand, and the minute the piece is removed from between the boards it will start to dry and wrinkle again. For small pieces where the veneer can be glued on before it starts to wrinkle, this method is fine.

A better way to treat hard-to-handle veneer is by using the following mixture: two parts Cascamite powder, one part flour, three parts water, one-and-a-half parts glycerin and one part alcohol. Mix the Cascamite and flour together, and add the water slowly so the mixture doesn't lump. Slowly add the glycerin and alcohol. Apply this mixture generously to both sides of the veneer or immerse the veneer in it. Then stand or hang the veneer on end until it is dry to the touch.

Clamp the veneer between two flat boards with three or four sheets of newspaper on each side to make it flat. After two hours, if the temperature in the room is about 70° F, replace the damp newspaper with dry. If left too long, the paper will stick or the veneer might mold. Put the veneer and fresh paper back between the two boards and clamp down. After three or four hours, remove the newspaper and put the veneer back between the boards without paper. Apply light pressure. The veneer should dry in a day. It will shrink a little, but it will still be flexible enough to use without cracking.

Keep the veneer between the boards until you use it. If more than one sheet of veneer from the same flitch has to be flattened, put the sheets on top of each other and double the layer of newspaper in between. After treatment, the veneer will be flexible and handle like regular veneer.

When veneering is done right, the type of veneer used should not make any difference. But regardless of how you treat them, burl and crotch veneer will eventually crack. This is because the grain is going in all directions and in some places it is end grain. Although I know of no way to prevent cracking, there is a way to postpone it. This is by sizing the veneer after it has been applied to its base with very thin hot glue. Experience will teach you how thin to make the sizing. An exact formula is impossible to give because the consistency of hot glue changes constantly as the water in it evaporates, but one part glue to two parts hot water is about right. Check the glue for proper consistency as explained on p. 122.

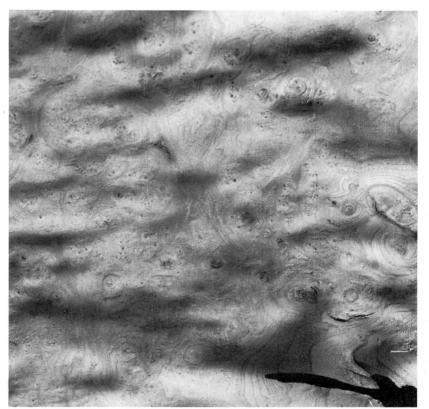

1

Before applying the sizing, scrape the veneer and sand it with 80-grit sandpaper. Use the palm of your hand to rub the sizing into the veneer. Wipe off any excess glue from the surface.

When the glue is completely dry, which usually takes about 24 hours, lightly scrape the veneer again, sand it with 80 grit and finish sanding with fine paper. The sizing will not discolor the veneer or interfere with the finish. By the way, rosewood will crack eventually, but it takes a long time and I'm not sure that even glue sizing will help.

A coat of glue sizing is also used in veneering end grain, to seal the pores of the wood. Let the sizing dry completely and then apply the veneer, using hot glue. Either hammer-veneer or use clamps. If the wood is soft, such as poplar or basswood, it might be better to size the ends twice, because the first coat will soak in.

When veneering end grain, never position the grain of the veneer across the width of the board **(2)**. The board and veneer will expand and contract in different directions and the veneer will loosen. Have the grain of the veneer going up and down with the thickness of the board if you can. Also, don't veneer the end of any board over ¾ in. thick. When the board changes in thickness, the veneer will come loose.

Glue sizing is also good for repairing cracked veneer when refinishing veneered pieces. Here the sizing should be thicker than usual. Equal parts of glue and hot water will be about right. Before removing the old finish, give it a coat of sizing and rub it in with the palm of your hand. Go across any cracks so you'll fill them. When the sizing dries it will pull down the veneer. After this kind of treatment, the veneer will usually stay down because it is old and will not move as much. When the glue is completely dry, remove the old finish with a cabinet scraper. Do not use a finish remover because it could dissolve the glue. □

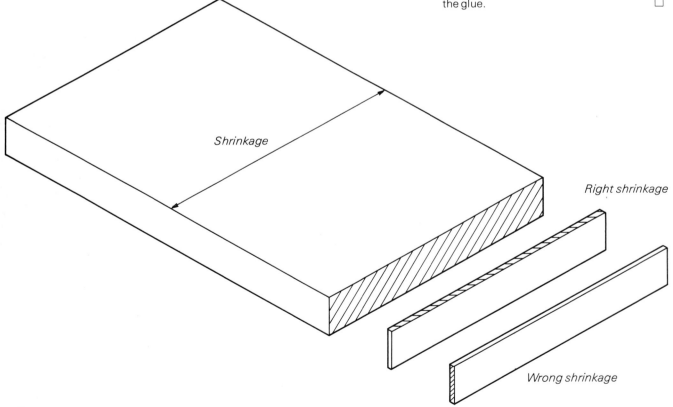

Shrinkage

Right shrinkage

Wrong shrinkage

2

Preparing Veneer

If sheets of veneer have to be pressed on with clamps or in a veneer press, they have to be joined and taped together first.

To get a straight edge on short pieces of veneer, clamp them between two straight boards **(1)**. You can put as many pieces between the boards as you like. Then trim one edge with a jointer plane **(2)** or run it over a jointer. Reclamp the boards, flipping the veneer over if both edges are to be joined.

To get a straight edge on long pieces, you can make a clamping jig that will hold the veneer tightly while it is being planed **(3,4)**. This particular jig is 6 ft. long but you can make it any length. It will last a long time. The two 2x3s can be used over and over again, but the two 1-in. boards in the center should be replaced when worn.

1

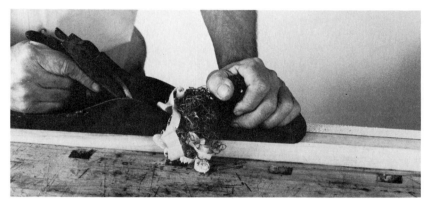

2

3

½" threaded dowel with handle

½" bolt with wing nut and washer

1" boards

6' 0".

Screwed to 2x3

4

Here **(5)** the jig is apart. One board is screwed to a 2x3 but the other is loose. A bolt in each end clamps the ends of the jig together **(6)**. In the top 2x3 there are three wooden screws with handles to put pressure on the center **(7)**.

Tap dies **(8)** for threading wood are available in different sizes. A good set of dies is a little more expensive but does a much better job than a cheaper set. When threading a dowel, be sure it is not too big for the die because the threads will break. Sand dowels that are too big to the correct size using a drill press.

Drill a hole for the female thread with a drill bit that is a hair smaller than the final size you want **(9)**. In this case I used a $\frac{7}{16}$-in. bit for a $\frac{1}{2}$-in. hole. Then I threaded the hole. If you have trouble with the threads breaking, you can fill the hole with linseed oil and empty it before threading.

The wooden thread joint **(10)** is strong, good for pieces that have to be assembled and disassembled repeatedly.

5

6

7

8

9

10

Once you've got straight edges on the pieces of veneer, you have to hold them together for gluing. It's a bad idea to use masking tape on the front of the veneer because the fibers might come up when you pull off the tape **(11)**. I used to use masking tape on the back of the veneer to be joined **(12)** and then flip the piece over and glue gum tape on the front. When the gum tape was dry, I removed the masking tape from the back. I found, however, that if I made the gum tape too wet, the veneer would expand and overlap.

I'm now back to doing it the way I learned as an apprentice. I line up the joints and keep the veneer from overlapping with very fine nails or brads. Then I glue on gum tape **(13)**. Wet it, but don't soak it — that's the key.

Use a cabinet scraper to remove the gum tape **(14)** after the veneer has been applied. You could remove the tape as soon as it comes out of the veneer press by soaking it with water and peeling it off, but I prefer to use a cabinet scraper because it is faster, safer and less messy. □

11

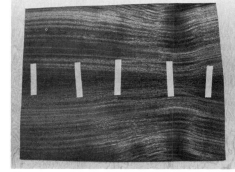

12

13

14

1

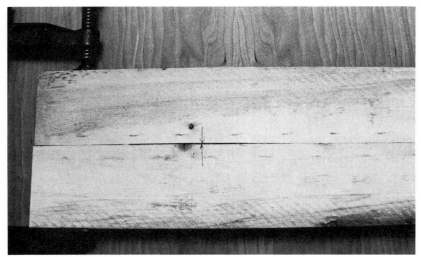

2

3

4

Veneering with Clamps

First I will explain veneering both sides of a ground surface without a commercially made veneer press, because very few craftsmen have one and it isn't really necessary for occasional veneer work. With some pieces of plywood and hand clamps, you can easily glue down veneer.

If the piece to be veneered is too wide for a clamp to reach its center, you will need to make a few sets of clamping boards to get the necessary pressure there. Plane the boards to a slight taper on the edges **(1)**. Make the taper even, so when the two pieces are clamped at the ends, the pressure will be uniform all along the joint **(2)**. An uneven taper will cause uneven pressure **(3)**. This is a good technique, but never veneer more than three pieces at the same time, because you will not get enough pressure.

Spread the glue on one side of the ground surface and apply the veneer, tacking it with veneer pins or tiny brads at each end in the center **(4)** to prevent it from sliding when pressure is applied. Don't tack the veneer in the corners because that will cause it to wrinkle when it tries to expand.

The piece will be clamped between two boards **(5)**, but first put down some paper onto one of them **(6)** so if any glue leaks, the veneer won't stick to the wrong thing. Put the piece, veneer side down, on the paper, and apply glue to the other side. Tack down the other piece of veneer, put on some paper and then cover with the other board.

Clamp the tapered pieces to the board, one piece on the top and one on the bottom **(7)**. Here I used two sets. Don't tighten the clamps too hard, and be sure that the pressure is in the center.

Now clamp boards at each end — they don't have to be tapered because a clamp can easily put pressure in the middle of the end **(8)**. Applying pressure to the center first gives the glue a chance to move out toward the edges and allows the veneer to expand. If the ends were clamped first, the glue would be trapped and the veneer would wrinkle. Up to this point work as fast as you can, but now give the glue a couple of minutes to ooze out. Then tighten up the clamps a little at a time.

Put the side clamps on the end boards **(9)**, making sure that the pressure is still mainly in the center. Slowly tighten all the clamps until the pressure is uniform throughout.

Leave the veneer clamped up for the amount of time recommended by the manufacturer of the type of glue that you use **(10)**. ☐

5

6

8

7

9

10

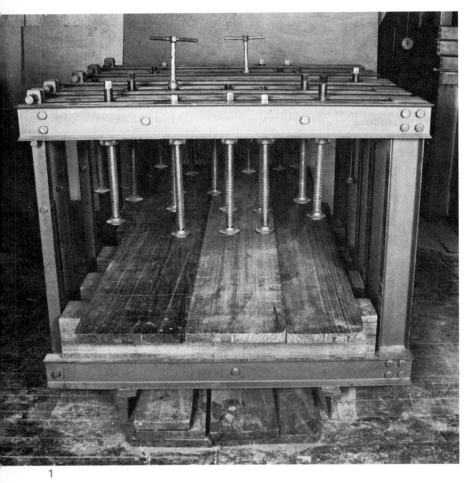

1

2

3

The Veneer Press

A commercially made veneer press is expensive but a worthwhile investment if you do much veneering, laminating or bending. This press **(1)** has five sections, so it can be used to veneer 4x8 sheets of plywood without the sections being more than 24 in. apart — the maximum distance that allows good pressure. Each section is movable from front to back; the screws on each section are movable from side to side.

This press is extra large (36 in. high and 50 in. wide) so it can be used with large jigs when bending plywood. For regular veneering, I put 7-in. by 7-in. blocks in the bottom of the press to raise the floor. On top of the blocks rest 1¾-in. thick planks. Soak the planks in oil so they won't warp and glue won't stick to them, but let the oil dry before using them.

Place the piece to be veneered in the press so that its end is flush with the press edge and position the sections. You can position the sections by eye or by first standing the piece to be veneered up against the side of the press **(2)**. Now position the screws. Always try to use an uneven number so you can clamp the center first. Place the screws so that the two outside ones are inside the edges of the piece to be veneered **(3)**, then remove the piece from the press.

On top of the planks, put a piece of plywood or particleboard. The planks and plywood will distribute the pressure uniformly among the sections. Put newspaper on top of the plywood so the veneer won't stick to it if glue should bleed through.

When you put the piece to be veneered in the press, make sure it lines up with the screws you have positioned **(4)**. Handle the veneer and the glue the same way as when using hand clamps. Cover the veneer with newspaper **(5)**.

If more than one piece of the same size is going to be veneered, separate the layers with a piece of plywood that is larger than the pieces being veneered **(6)**, and cover it with newspaper. Never put the pieces to be veneered directly on top of each other. The surface might be uneven, and if the pieces are not aligned exactly, the edges will not be glued properly. Continue stacking until all the pieces to be veneered are in the press **(7)**.

4

5

6

7

8

9

10

A final piece of plywood or particleboard goes on top of the stack **(8)**. All the plywood used should be smooth, because defects or debris will ruin the work. Then the stack is finished up with a 1¾-in. thick plank **(9)** and pieces of smooth, parallel 4x4s **(10)** to ensure that the pressure will be even. Here two are stacked on top of each other so the screws can reach.

Tighten up the center row of screws a little at a time. From the time you start spreading the glue until this point, work as fast as possible, but now slow down to give the glue a chance to ooze out toward the edges. Continue tightening the center screws a little at a time, but don't overdo it.

Slowly follow up with the outer screws **(11)**. As you work, try to keep the pressure uniform. Each time you tighten the outer screws, return to the center screws and tighten them again.

Many times, veneering will take more than one person and you should always try to get help. But after the center screws are tightened, only one person should finish tightening the other screws so the same amount of muscle goes into each. Don't be in a hurry to tighten the outer screws because the glue might get trapped, which would cause the veneer to buckle.

11

After the veneer comes out of the press, clean the edges while the glue is still a little soft. Hit the ends of the veneer with a chisel **(12,13)** to break the fibers so the veneer will be easier to cut. Check the piece for air bubbles by tapping the surface lightly and listening for hollow spots. If you don't locate them and glue them down, they will show up when the finish is put on and will eventually crack. If you can't find any bubbles by tapping, here's a way to be certain there aren't any. Scrape and sand the veneer with 80-grit paper, then apply a little hot water to the surface and keep it damp for a while. The moisture won't hurt the glue, but it will cause the veneer to expand where the bubbles are **(14)**. Mark the spot and let the veneer dry.

Next slice the bubble, going with the direction of the grain, with a sharp knife. Lift up the edge and shoot some glue under the veneer with a hypodermic needle **(15)**. In this photo, the veneer is still wet for clarity. Then put on paper, a block and a clamp, and allow the glue to dry **(16)**.

Stack the veneered pieces so that air circulates around them and both sides dry evenly **(17)**. Although the glue is set and the veneer won't come loose, the glue is not dry when the pieces are removed from the press because no air has circulated between the layers. If one side is covered up, the side exposed to air will dry first, pulling the work into a concave shape.   □

12

13

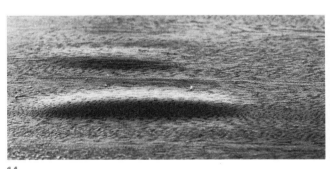

14

15

16

17

1

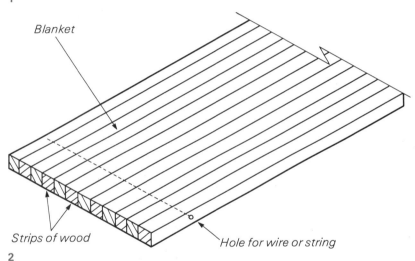

Blanket

Strips of wood

Hole for wire or string

2

Bending Plywood

In industry, bent plywood is made exactly like flat plywood, except a two-part form has to be made for the curve. Before you can make the form, which consists of a series of ribs nailed to slats, you have to make a full-size drawing of the actual piece you are going to bend. This drawing also includes the form blankets plus the ⅛-in. plywood facings that protect the face veneers. Build the blankets first.

The blankets are made out of many strips of wood of the same thickness, in this case ⅝ in. by ¾ in. **(1)**. Two or three holes are drilled in exactly the same place in each strip, and a string or wire is run through to line them up perfectly **(2)**. When they are strung together, the strips make a flexible blanket that fits on the form and gives it strength lengthwise. Here **(3)** is a half of the form without the blanket, and with the blanket on **(4)**. A blanket is also necessary between the piece to be bent and the top half of the form.

The length of the blanket is not critical as long as it is about 1 in. longer than the form on each end. Blankets can be altered for many different forms by adding or subtracting strips. Make some extra strips when you're milling them and keep them handy.

When the blankets are made, assemble and measure the rest of your materials. Don't assume when you buy ⅛-in. plywood that that's what you get, because all plywood varies in thickness.

3

4

It makes sense to build up the core of the piece you want to bend from thin plywood, not layers of veneer. It costs a bit more in materials, but you save labor and time. Italian poplar is best, as it bends easily and can be soaked in water for severe bends. If you do lay up the core from veneer, use perforated gum tape to join the interior layers. This tape is thinner than regular gum tape so it won't show up in the laminates, and glue can penetrate through the holes.

For this core I used six pieces of ⅛-in. plywood **(5)**. On each side of the core there is a ¹⁄₂₈-in. face veneer followed by a piece of ⅛-in. plywood on each side and finally the ⅝-in. blankets. The plywood evens out the pressure and prevents the sharp corners of the blankets from marring the veneer. The simplest way to add all this is to stack the pieces and measure them. These measure 2⁵⁄₁₆ in. The outside radius of the piece to be bent is 40 in.; the inner and outer radii on the drawing are the radii of the male and female parts of the bending form, respectively.

Usually I glue up the core first and glue on the face veneer later; it's easier to glue and cut the core to size and apply the edge facings before applying the face veneer. If a bend is complicated, it's sometimes good to glue the face veneers on the outside pieces of plywood before laminating the curve in the form, but be sure to get the pieces into the form the same day you get them out of the press, before the glue gets too dry.

Making the form After you've made the drawing, you're ready to make the form. Plan to make it about 1 in. wider and longer than the finished piece to ensure enough pressure on the ends. More than 1 in. is not good. Maximum distance between ribs should never be more than 6 in.

First nail together the pieces of plywood that will be the ribs of the form. In this case, I used eight pieces of ¾-in. plywood **(6)**, marked so I could keep them in the same order throughout the building process. Make sure the plywood lines up and is square.

Glue the drawing directly to the plywood with rubber cement **(7)** and mark the dadoes for the slats that will keep the ribs in place. Mark the centerline on the ends of the form as a reference for squaring up the bent piece and cutting it to width. Bandsaw out the curve, using the widest blade possible, to give a more even cut and fewer bumps and flat spots. When you saw, remember to split the line, keeping the kerf on the waste side.

6

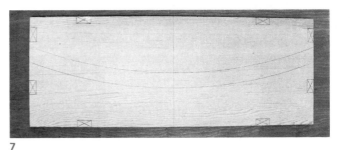

7

Six pieces of ⅛" plywood = ¾"

¹⁄₂₈" face veneer

⅛" plywood

⅝" blankets

40", radius of piece to be bent

40¾", radius of female half of bending form

38½", radius of male half of bending form

5

8

A two-part circle-cutting jig makes band-sawing accurate curves easy. To make the first part of the jig, cut into a piece of plywood so that its edge is flush with the back edge of the bandsaw table **(8)**. Clamp the plywood to the table and draw a line even with the sawblade teeth down its center. Measuring from the blade, mark the radius of the curve to be cut on that line, and then drill a hole there for a nail or dowel pivot. In this case the radius is 19 in. **(9)**.

Now make the second part of the jig. The first step is to make a thing that looks like a miter gauge **(10)**. Mark its center and the center of the piece you want to cut. Screw the two pieces together, matching up the lines. Mark the radius of the curve to correspond with the radius on the first part of the jig **(11)**.

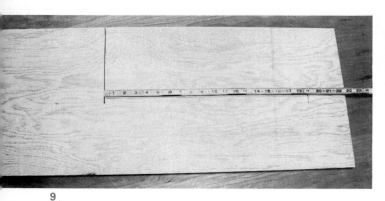

9

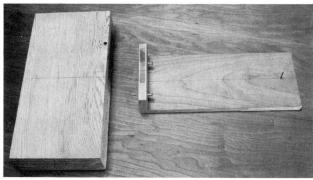

10

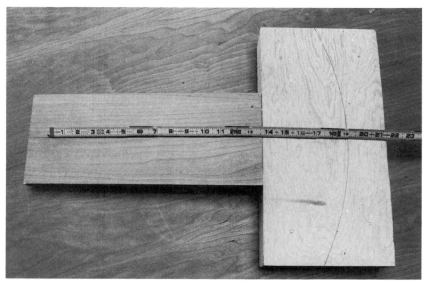

11

Place the assembly on the bandsaw, align the radii and put a nail through. Start the saw and cut **(12,13)**.

The curve will come out perfectly **(14)**, with no bumps or flat spots. The same jig can be used over again for different radii, so don't throw it away.

For cutting bigger pieces where the full depth of the saw throat is needed, the first part of this jig could be bolted to the bandsaw table. Drill two holes in the left side of the bandsaw tabletop and tap them for two flathead stove bolts.

12

13

14

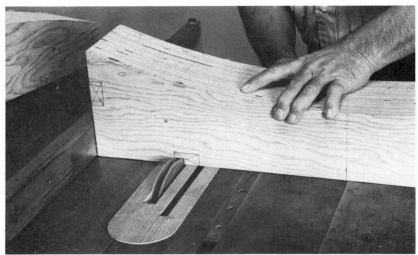

15

16

Now cut the grooves for the slats on both halves of the form, using a table saw with a dado head **(15, 16)**. The slats should fit snugly **(17)**. When all the cuts are made, separate the pieces of plywood, keeping them in order **(18)**, and mark all the slats where the ribs are going to be **(19)**. Assemble the form by nailing the slats to the ribs **(20)**. When the slats on the bottom are in, and you're ready to nail on the ones for the edges, make sure the ribs are square **(21)**.

17

18

19

20

21

22

Next, put the male and female halves of the form together **(22)**. Make sure the ribs line up with each other. Notice that the curves have different radii **(23)**. Two curves were cut on the block and the waste was removed.

If the curves of a form are not sections of a circle, you will need guide blocks to ensure that the halves of the form fit together properly **(24)**. If the halves do not line up exactly, the form will exert uneven pressure. Glue and screw two blocks or cleats to both ends of one half of the form, and glue and screw one block to both ends of the other half so that it will slide in between the first two.

23

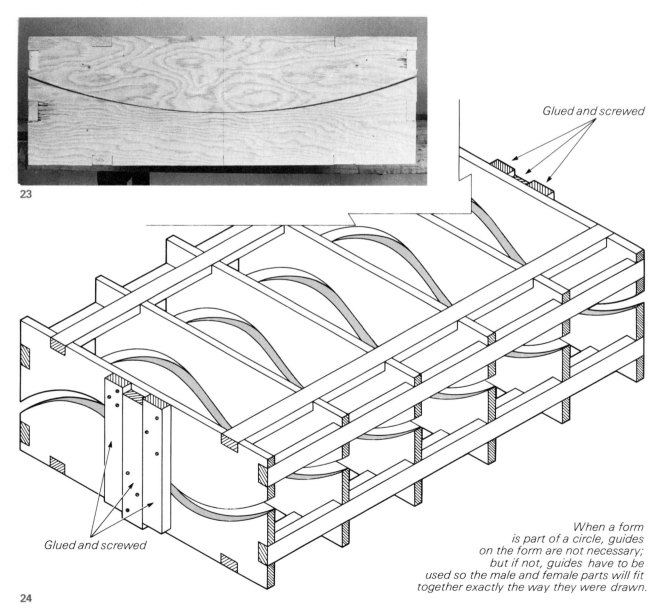

Glued and screwed

Glued and screwed

When a form is part of a circle, guides on the form are not necessary; but if not, guides have to be used so the male and female parts will fit together exactly the way they were drawn.

24

Forming the bend   Now the form is finished and ready to be used. You should assemble all necessary materials before you start to spread any glue. The selection and use of glue for bent plywood is the same as it is for flat. Once you've gotten the glue on, remember to tack the layers of plywood in the centers of the ends to prevent slipping. Before you clamp up, be certain that the centerlines of the form parts match up.

If you don't have a veneer press, place the form on two heavy planks to keep it from sagging **(25)**. Then put straight 2x4s across it. Here I used four 2x4s on the top and two 2x4s on the bottom, then I put another 2x4 in the center on the top.

Put a couple of pieces of veneer under the center of the 2x4 running lengthwise to make sure that there will be adequate pressure there **(26,27)**. This is faster than tapering (p. 140).

Clamp the top 2x4 first, then put the rest of the clamps on — but don't tighten them too much. Don't put too much pressure on the edges at first, because the glue must have a chance to squeeze out from the center. Work from the center outward, always returning to the center clamps each time you've tightened the outer clamps. Continue until the halves of the form are pressed together tightly and glue is squeezed out along the edges. Make sure that all the clamps have the same amount of pressure.

25

26

27

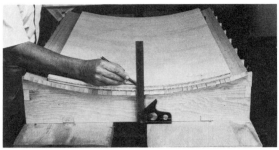

28

The glue will usually dry after about 24 hours, depending on room temperature. After the clamps come off, transfer the centerline of the form to the piece at both ends before moving it **(28)**. Then draw a reference line for squaring and cutting the piece to width **(29)**. From the reference line, mark both edges **(30)**. With a straightedge, connect the two points **(31)** and bandsaw down the line.

29

30

31

To cut the plywood to width, screw a block of wood to the fence of the table saw for the straight edge to rest upon **(32)**. You can control the angle of the edge being cut by varying the height of the fence block or by tilting the sawblade. Cut the edge oversize, then turn the piece around and cut the first edge to exact width.

To square the end, clamp a thin piece of wood to the concave side of the plywood. Square it up, draw a line **(33,34)**, and bandsaw it out.

Using a table saw, cut the plywood to length **(35)**. Put the end you just bandsawed against the fence and cut the other end, then turn the piece around to finish-trim the squared-up end. If you remembered to make your piece a little longer than necessary, you will now be cutting off the brad marks at both ends.

Use the same methods to apply face veneer to curved stock as to straight. Clamp the 2x4s going lengthwise first, and then slowly apply pressure to the rest of the clamps. Remember, give the glue a chance to squeeze out toward the ends.

If I had to make a large quantity of bent-plywood pieces, I would get them made in a place that specializes in that sort of thing, because it probably would be cheaper than doing it myself. □

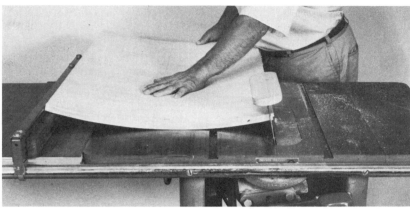

32

33

34

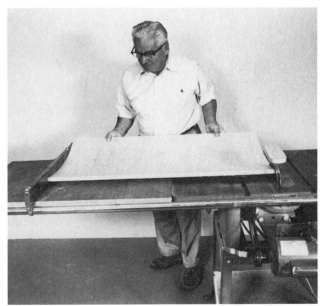

35

1

2

3

Sandbag-Veneering

If you don't want to make a two-part form, sandbags can be used to veneer pieces that are not flat. For this operation you need clamps, sandbags and a caul.

A caul is a piece of wood that goes on top of the sandbag (this is also where the clamps go). The caul doesn't have to fit the concavity of the piece to be veneered exactly, as the sandbag will distribute even pressure **(1)**.

With this technique, use hot glue whenever possible. Hot glue is strong and sets fast, and because the veneer is clamped down before the glue starts melting, it cannot expand as it absorbs the moisture.

Put the glue only on the piece to be veneered, not on the veneer. Let the glue cool, and then apply the veneer with a piece of paper on top so the sandbag won't stick to the veneer if any glue bleeds through.

Before putting on the glue, heat the sandbag, half-filled with fine sand, in an electric frying pan or in an oven set to 220° F. Make sure to sift the sand before putting it in the bag. Then place the sandbag on the veneer, spreading out the sand evenly **(2)**.

Put the caul on and clamp it down as quickly as possible **(3)**. As soon as the sand is cold, the glue will hold down the veneer and the clamps can be removed. Scrape with a gooseneck scraper blade and sand using a blackboard eraser for a block, and you are all done.

Sandbags can also be used over convex surfaces and with forms. Large forms can be made out of plaster of paris.   □

Inlay
Chapter 7

Inlaying with an Electric Router

Many people confuse inlay and marquetry, but they are two completely different techniques. I like inlay because it is easier than marquetry to design and do, and usually the grain of the wood doesn't have to be chosen as carefully. I prefer to use wood with straight grain for inlay work, because it is less distracting and better emphasizes the shape of the simple forms I like to work with. Marquetry doesn't interest me much, although sometimes I do simple abstractions on the tops of boxes. I am definitely not interested in commercially available pictures such as pretty roses.

When doing inlay work, there are two rules to follow. First, do not inlay solid wood into plywood, as the inlay will crack when it dries and shrinks. Second, when inlaying into solid wood, make sure that the grain of the inlay goes in the same direction as the piece to be inlaid. If you inlay a piece going against the grain or at an angle, the inlay will eventually be pushed out by wood movement.

The oldest way to inlay wood is to make the inlay, put it on the piece to be inlaid, scribe around it, chisel out the recess and smooth the bottom of the recess with a router plane. An easier way is to use a portable electric router with a template guide and a bushing. The idea here is to rout the recess with the bushing pressed onto the template guide, then to remove the bushing before routing the inlay. Thus, provided the walls of the bushing are the same as the diameter of the router bit, recess and inlay will end up the exact same size. The advantage of this method is that the same template makes both inlay and recess. The bit will cut on one side of the line with the bushing on the template guide, and on the other side of the line with the bushing removed. The drawing **(1)** shows the relationship of the template guide, bushing and bit.

For small inlays with fine detail, I use a ⅛-in. router bit. The size of the template guide is not important — I use the smallest one that will fit the bit I am using. Remember that the walls of the bushing must be the same thickness as the diameter of the bit. It is not difficult to make your own bushing nor is it expensive to have one made, but the bushing has to press-fit the guide so it won't fall off when you use it.

The drawback to this technique is that the corners of the inlay can't come to a sharp point, but of course they could be chiseled out afterward and the point of the inlay fitted by hand.

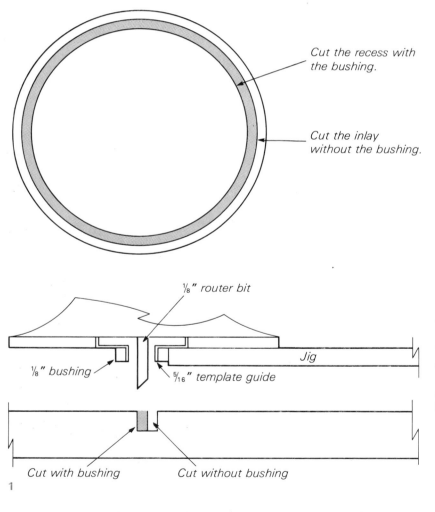

Cut the recess with the bushing.

Cut the inlay without the bushing.

⅛" router bit

⅛" bushing

⁵⁄₁₆" template guide

Jig

Cut with bushing   Cut without bushing

1

Here I am using a ⅛-in. router bit, a ⅛-in. bushing and a ⁵⁄₁₆-in. template guide. This photograph **(2)** shows the template guide without the bushing and this one **(3)** with the bushing on.

To guide the router, you will need a jig that is larger than the inlay to allow for the template guide and the bit **(4)**. I find that ¼-in. plywood works fine for the jig. To determine how much bigger than the inlay to make the jig, measure the distance from the cutting edge of the bit to the outside of the template guide; in this case, ³⁄₃₂ in. Add this measurement to the diameter of the bit, in this case, ⅛ in. The sum is ⁷⁄₃₂ in., so the radius of the jig must be ⁷⁄₃₂ in. larger than the inlay **(5)**.

2

3

4

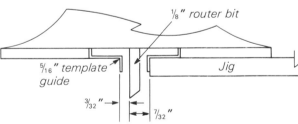

5

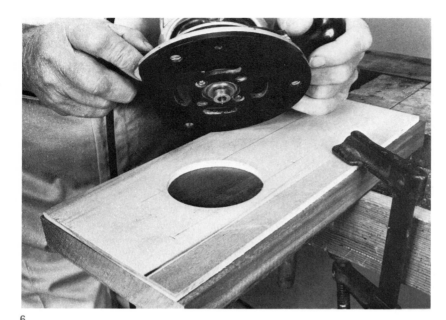

6

After making the jig, clamp it to the board that is going to receive the inlay **(6)**. Put the bushing on the template guide and set the router bit to the right depth, about ³⁄₁₆ in. into the wood. Start the router in about the center of the jig and move out toward the edge until the bushing touches it **(7)**. Then, with the bushing following the jig, cut all the way around. Rout clockwise, so the bit will push the bushing against the jig. If you rout counterclockwise, the bit will push the bushing away from the jig. It's a good idea to rout on a scrap piece first, just to make sure you're going the right way.

After the circle is cut, remove the rest of the wood in the center **(8)**. If the recess is large and there's too much wood to remove with the small bit, use a larger one. If you do this, it's a good idea to cut out the inlay before changing to the larger bit.

7

8

Now cut the inlay. The first step is to remove the bushing from the template guide. Then clamp the jig to the board from which the inlay is going to be cut.

Cutting the inlay usually requires two people, unless you are using a plunge router (p. 163). With the bit retracted, position the router in the jig, holding the template guide against the edge of the jig. Start the router and have somebody lower the bit to the desired depth **(9)**. This is a safe technique, especially when using a small bit. With one person holding the router tight against the jig, it is the same as using a drill press or a plunge router.

Follow the edge of the jig to rout out the inlay. Make sure to move the router clockwise, or else you'll be in trouble. When you are finished, turn off the router and let it stop before removing it.

Here **(10,11)** the inlay is cut and ready to be removed from the board.

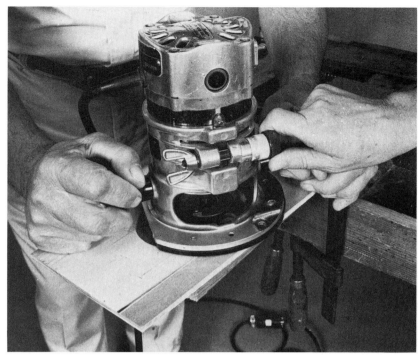

9

10

11

12

13

Now mark the desired thickness of the inlay, set the fence on the table saw and cut out the inlay **(12)**. You could also use a bandsaw. Keep the inlay on the outside of the saw so it can fall free after it is cut **(13)**. Never allow it between the fence and the sawblade, where it would be trapped and might get damaged.

Don't try to cut an inlay from a board that is the exact same thickness you want; if you did, the inlay would come loose the minute the cut was completed, and the router bit would chew it up. If you have to use a board of exactly the same thickness, glue it to another board using rubber cement or hot glue with brown paper between.

When the piece is cut out, it should fit perfectly. Just glue it in and sand it flush **(14)**.

This technique has many decorative applications, especially when you use circles of different diameter. I also use inlaid circles to repair imperfections in wood, with the advantage that you can move the inlay around in the recess to match the grain. (For small imperfections, of course, you can use a plugcutter and drill press to cut circles.) ☐

14

Inlaying with a Plunge Router

Inserting a panel into a frame having edges that are not straight is hard to do with hand tools, but with a plunge router, template guide and bushing, it is easy and accurate. Plunge routing lets you begin and end a cut in the middle of a piece of stock without having to lower or lift the base from the work. With the motor running, you can lower the bit into the wood by simply pushing down on the handles.

I finally broke down and bought a Makita 2¾-HP 3600 B plunge router, which I should have done years ago. It has many advantages over other routers I have used and is both well designed and made. The body is attached to the rectangular base by two ⅞-in. diameter steel posts. These fit into sleeves in the body that can slide up and down on the posts (against spring tension) and be locked at any height. The switch can be worked without having to move your hand from the handle **(1)**, but it's not located right on the handle where you might turn it on accidentally while picking up the router. The body is locked on the posts by a latching lever instead of a knob, and you can reach this lever to raise or lower the bit without having to take your hand off the handle **(2)**.

1

2

An adjustable knob on top of the router **(3)** stops the upward travel and also controls the depth of cut for ordinary routing. To set the depth, simply press the button, which is a half nut, and slide the rod to the approximate setting **(4,5)**. For final adjustment, release the button so that the rod can be worked like a screw. The stop block of this router can be set to two different depths **(6,7)**, necessary when making a haunched mortise, for example. But you can control the depth of cut when plunge routing without using these stops. Just turn on the router, release the lock lever, push the bit down to the desired depth and lock it.

This router is also good for mortising, which I explain how to do on p. 167.

3

4

5

The first step in inserting an inlay panel into a frame with curved edges is to make an oversize jig. Here I am using a ⅜-in. template guide and a ¼-in. bit. The distance from the cutting edge of the bit to the outside of the template guide is ¹⁄₁₆ in. This plus the bit equals ⁵⁄₁₆ in., so that is how much bigger than the inlay all around to make the jig.

When the jig is made, nail it at the corners to the piece from which you are going to cut the inlay **(8)**. Keep a piece of plywood underneath the inlay so that you don't cut into the bench. Glue the inlay material to the plywood using rubber cement or hot glue with brown paper between, so when the inlay is cut free it won't slip into the router bit and get damaged.

6

7

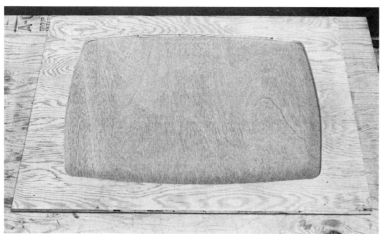

8

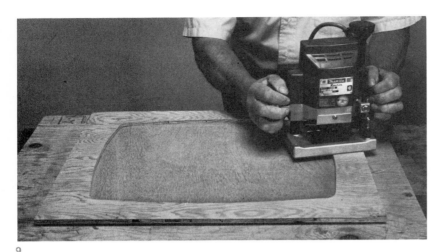

9

10

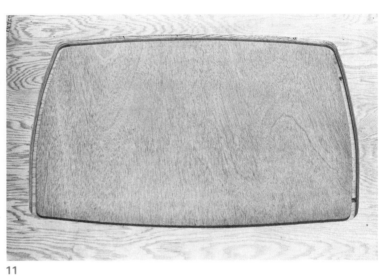

11

Now put the plunge router (without the bushing) on the jig **(9)**, start it and lower the bit — about ¼ in. into the wood should be safe. Start to cut, making sure to move clockwise **(10)**. (If you were to use a male jig instead of a female jig, you would have to move the router counterclockwise, because you'd be using the opposite side of the router.) Here the inlay is cut **(11)**.

Now place the jig on the frame. Be sure it is positioned properly, so the inlay won't be crooked. Clamp the ends **(12)** and rout the sides first, again moving the router clockwise. Remember to put the bushing on before you do this.

12

After the sides are routed, move the clamps one at a time and rout the ends **(13)**. Remove the rest of the wood with the plunge router.

Notice how perfectly the inlay fits into the frame **(14)**.

As I have said, the Makita plunge router is also excellent for use as a mortising machine, but a guide base, which is secured with one wing nut, has to be used **(15)**. A mortising machine is a very important piece of equipment, but it usually costs about $2400. By building a simple fixture for holding the stock and cutting the mortises with the router, you can have a mortising setup that works just as well as an expensive machine, but that costs only about $350.

13

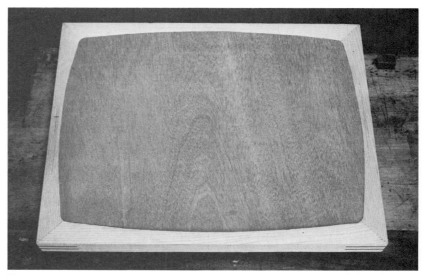

14

15

16

The mortising fixture I made looks like a big miter box **(16,17)**. Its length and depth can be varied to suit your needs, but its inside width should not be more than 3¼ in. or the router base will not rest on both sides. Make the bottom of the fixture from two pieces of ¾-in. plywood and make the sides from plywood, too, because solid wood might warp. Install lateral stops on the top edge of the inboard side of the fixture. The stops are slotted strips of wood grooved on their bottoms to fit over and slide along the edge. The slot in each stop rides around a screw, which you tighten when you determine the length of the mortise you want to cut. I use ³⁄₁₆-in. stove bolts to secure each stop. They are engaged by T-nuts embedded into the side of the fixture; ¼-in. hanger bolts (bolts having machine threads on one end and wood threads on the other) with wing nuts could also be used.

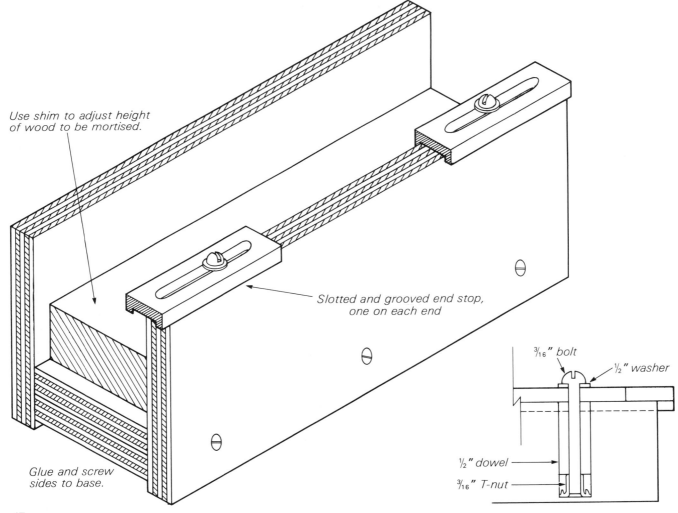

Use shim to adjust height of wood to be mortised.

Slotted and grooved end stop, one on each end

Glue and screw sides to base.

³⁄₁₆ " bolt

½ " washer

½ " dowel

³⁄₁₆ " T-nut

17

To cut the mortises in a piece of regular dimension, a straight table leg, for example, shim up the workpiece in the fixture so it's almost flush with the top edge **(18)**. Roughly center the area to be mortised in the middle of the fixture and clamp it to the side facing you. Set the stops to contact the router base so the bit can travel the full length of the mortise in one pass. With the fixture held in a vise, or secured to your bench some other way, set the fence on the router the right distance from the bit and butt the base against the left-hand stop.

Switch on the power, release the lock lever and lower the bit into the wood. For a ⅜-in. bit, a ¼-in. depth of cut should be safe.

Then pull the router to the right **(19)**, so the rotation of the bit will hold the fence against the side of the fixture, which will give you a good straight cut. If you were to start at the right-hand stop and push the router to the left, you could get an uneven cut.

Mortising is best done by making several passes to reach final depth, cutting ¼ in. to ⅜ in. deep with each pass, depending on the density of the wood and on the size and kind of bit you're using. All this may sound complicated, but you will be surprised at how fast it works. I think this system is faster and cleaner-cutting than a hollow-chisel mortiser. Here is the finished mortise **(20)**.

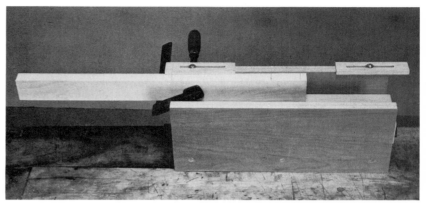

18

19

20

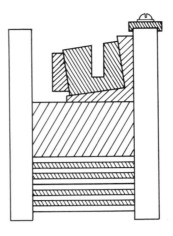

21

For cutting angled mortises in regular stock, like those in chair legs to receive stretchers and rails, you will have to make angled shims that will hold the stock in the right relation to the bit **(21)**, as you would have to for any mortising machine. To mortise curved pieces, a chair back, for instance, bandsaw a piece to fit the side of the curve opposite the cut and use it to support the stock when clamped in the fixture **(22,23)**. You can place the curved shim underneath the stock for mortising on one side. To mortise the adjoining side, support the stock from the inboard side of the fixture, using the same curved shim and a flat support on the bottom. Here **(24)** both mortises are cut.

For general mortising, two-flute straight-face carbide bits will do a good job. High-speed steel bits will work, but will get dull faster and cut a little slower. The Makita plunge router comes with ¼-in. and ⅜-in. adapter sleeves for its ½-in. collet, so you can use different bit sizes and cut mortises of almost any width and up to 2⅜-in. deep. ☐

22

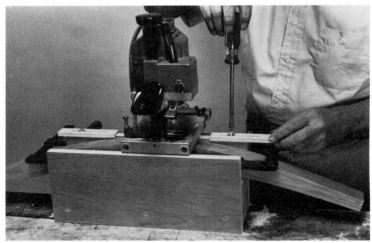

23

24

Finishing
Chapter 8

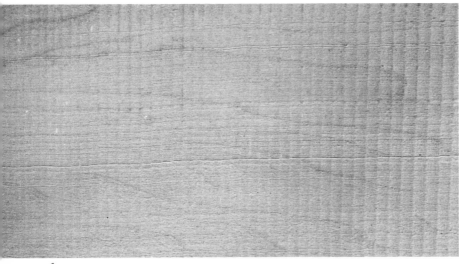

1

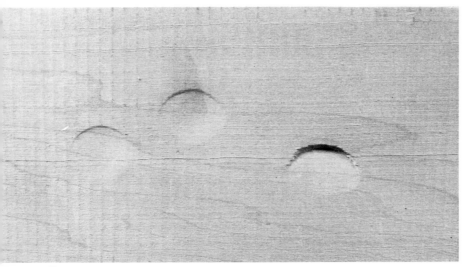

2

Preparation

Finishing is an important part of making fine furniture. You can build a beautiful piece, but if the finish is bad, both beauty and value will be lessened.

Finishing starts the instant you pick up the smoothing plane, which has to be used first if the piece is made of solid wood. (If the wood is curly or bird's-eye maple, use a cabinet scraper, p. 35, instead.) The plane removes the small marks left by jointer and thickness-planer knives **(1)**, which will show up after the finish is on. If the knives are dull, the marks will be even more noticeable.

To demonstrate how knife marks can swell up and stand out, I made three hammer marks **(2)** on the surface of a piece of wood. The two on the left are about $\frac{1}{16}$ in. deep; the one on the right is about $\frac{1}{8}$ in. deep.

I planed the wood **(3)** so that the two marks on the left felt flush with the surface but were still visible, and then I sanded **(4)**. After sanding, the marks on the left were almost gone, but the mark on the right was still half there **(5)**.

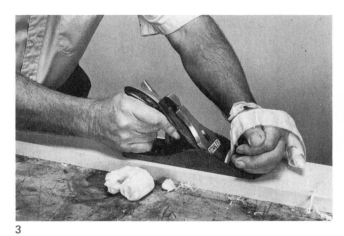

3

4

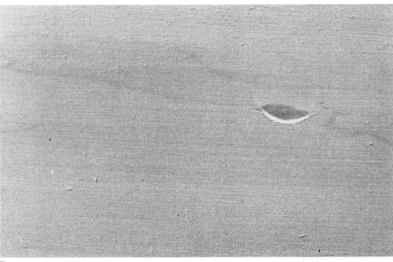

5

6

7

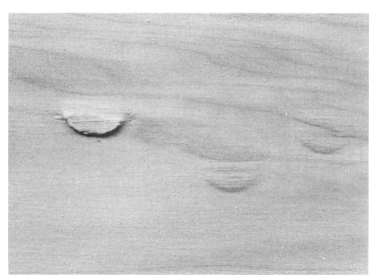

8

Next I applied water to the surface through a double layer of paper toweling **(6)**. (The bottle was filled with water, not rice wine.) Moving a warm iron over the paper toweling created steam **(7)** — remember that moisture and heat expand wood.

As you can see, even though the two $\frac{1}{16}$-in. hammer marks were flush after the board was planed and sanded, the moisture made the wood fibers raise above the surface **(8)**. The $\frac{1}{8}$-in. deep hammer mark, which was not planed flush, raised $\frac{1}{16}$ in. above the surface. The same thing would happen after the finish was put on.

So a good way to remove dents in wood before finishing is to apply steam and then plane the surface with a smoothing plane. Dents can also be raised with warm water put on the surface and allowed to dry, but for deep dents I recommend using steam.

Unless the wood has dents, I usually don't bother to raise the grain before finishing. The only exception is when I am going to use a water stain (p. 182).

After the wood is planed, use a scraper blade to remove the plane marks. This is much faster than sanding. Because the edge of a scraper blade is straight, it will make the surface perfectly level. Most people sand too much and waste time doing it.

When you are working on a piece, try to avoid denting or dropping it. Keep your bench clean; be sure there is no old glue on it, which will definitely dent the wood. Remember that every blemish creates more work for you to do later. □

Sanding

After scraping out the marks left by the smoothing plane, you're ready to sand the surface of the wood. For a sanding block I like to use a piece of cork approximately 4½ in. by 3 in. by 1⅜ in. **(1)**. It fits the hand and is just the right size for a quarter sheet of sandpaper. Cork is light and inexpensive, with a firm and flat, but not hard, surface. Fancy rubber sanding blocks with slots in each end to hold the sandpaper are too heavy and waste too much paper.

Don't use a knife, chisel or scissors to cut sandpaper. Just fold it **(2)** and tear it into quarters on a sharp edge **(3)**. Wrap a quarter of the sheet around the block so that it is off center **(4)**, not as shown here **(5)**. When the portion of the sandpaper you are using dulls, simply move an unused section over into its place. This way, more of the quarter sheet can be used.

1

2

3

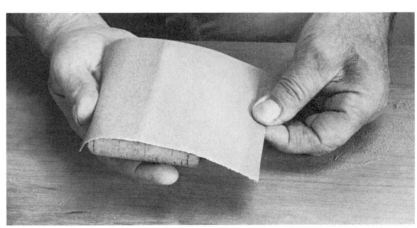

4

5

6

7

Although there are many different opinions on sanding, I prefer to use 80-grit and 120-grit paper for most work. For fine sanding, I use 180 grit. I am not an expert on sandpaper, but I have tried most kinds, and I prefer garnet open-coat D with paper backing. (Open coat simply means that only 60% to 80% of the surface of the paper is coated with abrasives, reducing the paper's tendency to clog. The letter refers to paper weight — D is medium weight.) Always sand with the grain or else scratches will show up when the finish goes on.

I have an oscillating sander **(6)** but hardly ever use it because it makes tiny circular scratches in the wood. Also, its base is soft, which can create an uneven surface. As you can see by the edges **(7)**, the mice like it. This type of sander is fine to use between coats if you have a lot of finishing to do.

A belt sander **(8)** is a good investment. It can ruin a piece faster than almost any other tool, but once you've learned how to use it correctly, it can be a big help. Belt sanders have a steel plate on the bottom **(9)** that keeps the surface even, and the mice won't eat it. I use mine all the time and usually can get away without using a smoothing plane first. Using an X-weight 60-grit belt, which is a heavy cloth, I run the sander 45° to the grain in one direction and then 45° in the opposite direction until the surface is flat. Then, using the same grit, I remove the angled sanding marks by going back and forth with the grain. I repeat the process with 80 grit and 120 grit, going with the grain. Lastly, I go over the surface with a sanding block and sandpaper, again using 80 grit first, then 120 grit. I finish up with 180 grit.

When you are using a belt sander, keep it flat on the surface. Rocking it from side to side could result in scratches or dips in the surface, which would show up after the finish has been applied **(10)**.

Make sure to move the sander all the way through a stroke from one end to the other. This is especially important when using the 120-grit belt. Let a third of the sanding plate stick out over the edge of the work before changing directions **(11)**. Going halfway and then turning back could result in scratches in the surface.　□

8

9

10

11

1

2

3

4

Filler

I never use commercial filler and sanding sealer because they cloud the wood and usually change color with age. The only time I use filler is to fill imperfections, and when I do, I make my own. Commercial Plastic Wood filler might match the color of your wood in the beginning, but as the wood gets darker, which it normally does, the Plastic Wood will stick out like a sore thumb.

To make your own filler, save the sanding dust from the particular piece you are working on. Then, if you are using a shellac or oil finish, mix the dust with 2-lb. cut liquid shellac so that it is the consistency of putty and use it to fill the imperfection. If you are going to lacquer the piece, mix the sanding dust with thinned lacquer. Or, if you're going to stain the piece, mix the sanding dust with either thin hot glue or Titebond diluted 50% with water.

Put enough filler on so that it can be sanded flush with the surface after it dries. Because the filler is made of the same wood it fills, it will fade with the wood. Making your own filler is cheaper than buying Plastic Wood; you also don't have to store all those cans.

Sometimes a beautiful piece of wood has loose knots or knotholes. To fill them so that they look natural, use stick shellac. It's easy to make stick shellac yourself. I'm sure my son, who is a volunteer fire chief, would not approve of the way I do it in the shop, but I feel it's perfectly safe. Just be sure that the shop is reasonably clean and no sawdust or shavings are next to the fire. Definitely do not make stick shellac in your finishing room.

To begin, put about a handful of orange shellac flakes **(1)** on a flat piece of metal and pour on about one tablespoon of alcohol **(2)**. Move the flakes around to spread the alcohol evenly, then stand back and light it with a match **(3)**. As the alcohol burns, it will melt the flakes. To make sure all the flakes melt, move them around with an old chisel or a piece of metal **(4)**.

When all the alcohol has burned off and the flakes have melted, form the shellac into a stick. Put motor oil on your hands first to protect them **(5,6)** and to prevent hot flakes from sticking to them. Then scrape the shellac off the plate with the chisel and start to form it **(7,8)**. This photograph **(9)** shows the finished stick.

5

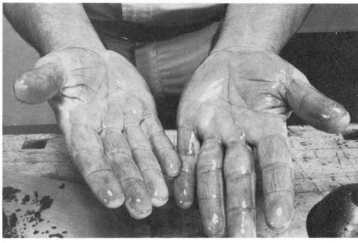

6

7

8

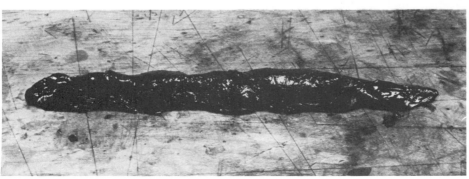

9

10

Here is a piece of walnut with a loose knot and a knothole **(10)**. To melt the stick shellac into them, you can use burning-in irons or hot knives, which are best for big jobs. I usually just use a match **(11)**.

While the shellac is still hot, force it all the way down with the back of a chisel or knife **(12,13)**, but moisten the back of the tool first to prevent the shellac from sticking to it. When the shellac has cooled, clean off the excess from the surface of the wood with a sharp chisel **(14)**.

Sand the shellac flush with the surface. When the piece is finished, the knots look natural **(15,16)**. □

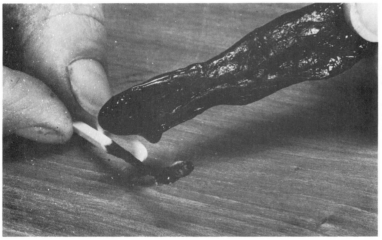

11

12

13

14

15

16

Staining

Wood with naturally beautiful color should not be stained. However, some wood can be tinted with a very weak stain to brighten its natural color. Stain is also sometimes used to blend sapwood with heartwood.

A good stain should penetrate the wood and resist fading. It should also be inexpensive. I like to use stains made from about 4 oz. (112 grams) of water-soluble aniline dye powder dissolved in about 1 gal. (3.8 liters) of hot (not boiling) water. Let the stain cool at room temperature before using.

Aniline dye powder is available in many colors, but the two best suited for most hardwoods are bismark brown (reddish brown) and nigrosine jet (black). Keep the powder in an airtight container so that it will not absorb moisture. To dissolve the powder, use water that is as clean as possible and free from iron and calcium — distilled water is safest. It's best to mix the amount of stain you need each time, because liquid stain will lose some of its color if stored too long. Never keep liquid stain in a metal container.

Before using water stain, always moisten the wood with warm water to raise the grain. When the wood dries, sand with fine sandpaper. If you don't do this, the grain will raise when the stain is applied, resulting in a fuzzy surface. Non-grain-raising stains are available in liquid form, and these seem to work fine, but I don't know how much the color will fade over time.

Water stain is fast and easy to apply, and it does not leave a heavy film on the wood. Apply the stain with a brush, after testing it on a scrap piece of wood. After two or three minutes, if you want a light color, wipe off the stain with a dry cloth; for a dark color, even out the stain with a dustbroom.

Don't use an oil finish over a water stain or any stain except a chemical stain, because the oil won't protect it. A shellac, lacquer or varnish finish must be used instead.

In Denmark in the 1930s, stain made from aniline dye powder was widely used, especially on less expensive furniture made of rotary-cut birch plywood. All kinds of tricks were used to disguise the plywood, such as imitating curly birch and maple with stains.

1

Once, when I was still an apprentice, I took a job refinishing a cabinet to make a little extra money. I thought the cabinet was made of curly maple, but when I started removing the finish, I found it was plain maple. You can imagine how I felt. Luckily, I knew an old painter who saved me by teaching me a lesson on how to fake it.

Use a water-based stain and apply it so that the color is fairly even **(1)**. Then take a damp cloth or chamois and twist it. For curly birch, don't twist too hard **(2)**; for curly maple, twist more **(3)**. Roll the cloth over the stain while it is still wet **(4,5)**. The raised part of the cloth will absorb some of the stain. However, in those areas where the cloth does not touch the surface, the stain will remain dark and will appear as curls there.

2

3

4

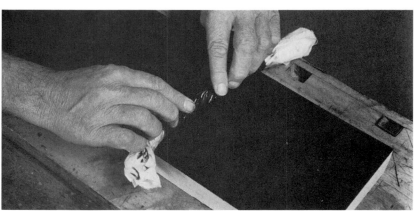
5

For a bird's-eye effect, dab the end of a sponge cloth, or a damp sponge, onto the surface **(6)**. A nonprofessional will find it very hard to tell if the finished product is real or not.

Another trick is imitating rosewood or other dark, heavily grained wood. Here **(7)**, I used a rosewood-colored, oil-based stain to flood the wood, and painted in the figure with a feather — the wing feather from a goose is best. Oil stain doesn't dry as fast and doesn't flow out as easily as water stain, so it's good for an application like this. But oil stain leaves a heavy film on the wood and usually I don't like to use it.

Alcohol-soluble aniline stains are not very fade-proof and I usually don't use them either. But they can be used to stain shellac and are often used in French polishing. Shellac mixed with nigrosine jet results in a black finishing material that was used in the French polishing of black pianos. When you use stain mixed with shellac for French polishing, however, it can take up to four weeks for the color to fade from your hands.

Chemical stains In the 1930s, staining was also often used for expensive furniture, but the wood was colored by chemical means. At that time, the chemicals were available from special paint stores, but today many of those chemicals are not easy to come by. Whether this is the cause or the effect, chemical staining has become a dying art.

Chemical stains are not stains in the usual sense of the word, because they work through chemical action. Therefore, they leave no film on the wood — a major advantage to using them. Chemical stains are also water-resistant, so you can use an oil finish over them, and they are virtually fade-proof. Chemical stains take more time to apply than stains made from aniline-dye powder, but the results are well worth it — you can get some fantastic colors.

A chemical stain must be applied in two steps. First there is a prestain, or mordant — such as tannic acid, pyrogallol, pyrocatechol or nitroso-b-napthol. The second stain, or afterstain, can be ammonia or salts of iron, cobalt, copper, chromium, manganese or nickel. There are many possible combinations of prestains and afterstains. The chart on the facing page gives some of them and the resulting colors.

Chemical stains take differently on different woods. (They even react differently with the heartwood and sapwood of the same wood.) On woods having tannic acid, such as oak, chemical stains will usually produce a darker color than on woods not having tannic acid. Softwoods take chemical stains well, but it is necessary to apply a wash of ammonia after staining to help the stain penetrate. On hardwoods, a wash of ammonia will often bring out new colors. You can mix ammonia with other afterstains, as long as no sediment results. Always experiment on scrap first.

Apply chemical stain with either a sponge or a brush. If using a sponge, protect your hands by wearing rubber gloves. If using a brush, make sure there is no metal piece holding the hairs.

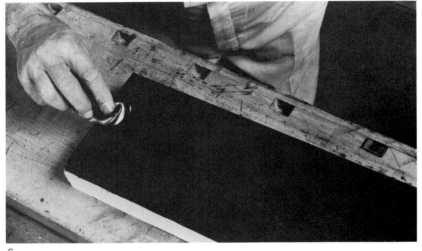

6

7

Allow at least 24 hours drying time between coats so the chemicals have time to work. It's a good idea to go over the stained surface with a cloth when the stain is dry or to sand it lightly between coats with 320-grit paper, to smooth out the surface. Never use steel wool between coats. Horsehair is good to use, as it is better for smoothing than a cloth and easier to use than sandpaper.

Ebonizing Here is a great black stain, but it must be used with an oil finish.

Mix together in a clean jar 3½ oz. (100 grams) of copper sulfate, 1¾ oz. (50 grams) of potassium chlorate and 22 oz. (615 grams) of hot distilled water. In another jar, mix 3½ oz. (100 grams) of aniline hydrochloride, 1⅖ oz. (40 grams) of ammonium chloride and 22 oz. (615 grams) of hot distilled water. To use, mix equal parts of the solutions together, but don't mix any more than you think you will need for each coat. Apply three coats with a sponge or brush, allowing 24 hours drying time in between coats. When the third coat is dry, smooth it with fine sandpaper, using linseed oil as a lubricant.

The first coat of this finish will look a little yellow, the second coat will look a little green, and the third coat will look very green. But don't get nervous, because the instant the oil touches the finish, it will turn a deep, beautiful black. After the stain dries, finish the piece with oil – tung, linseed or penetrating oil is okay. ☐

Colors resulting from combinations of prestains and afterstains.

Prestain	Afterstain *	Color
Tannic acid, 1¾ oz. (50 grams) per quart (liter) of hot distilled water	Ammonia	Golden brown
	Ferrous sulfate	Ivory black
	Cobaltous chloride	Golden brown
	Potassium dichromate	Cool brown
	Nickel chloride	Golden brown
Pyrogallol, 1¾ oz. (50 grams) per quart (liter) of hot distilled water	Ammonia	Chestnut brown
	Ferrous sulfate	Greenish black
	Cobaltous chloride	Brown
	Copper chloride	Dark reddish brown
	Potassium dichromate	Dark reddish brown
	Manganous dichloride	Honey brown
	Nickel chloride	Honey brown
Pyrocatechol, 1¾ oz. (50 grams) per quart (liter) of hot distilled water	Ammonia	Cool brown
	Ferrous sulfate	Bluish black
	Cobaltous chloride	Greenish brown
	Copper chloride	Greenish black
	Potassium dichromate	Brownish black
Nitroso-B-naphthol, ⅖ oz. (10 grams), and potassium hydroxide, ⅒ oz. (3½ grams), per quart (liter) of boiling distilled water	Ammonia	Gold
	Ferrous sulfate	Spring green
	Cobaltous chloride	Indian red
	Copper chloride	Burnt orange
	Potassium dichromate	Reddish orange
	Manganous dichloride	Lemon
	Nickel chloride	Orange

* To mix afterstain, dissolve ⅖ oz. (10 grams) of ferrous sulfate, cobaltous chloride, copper chloride, manganous dichloride or nickel chloride in a quart (liter) of hot distilled water. For potassium-dichromate stain, mix 7⁄10 oz. (20 grams) of the chemical in a quart (liter) of hot distilled water. Ammonia afterstain is simply 27% ammonia solution (available from chemical supply houses).

Finishing Materials

There are many different kinds of finishing materials. Each has advantages and disadvantages, and certain ones, like lacquer and varnish, are more difficult to use than others. Some finishes sit on the surface of the wood so you have to look through a film; others, such as oil, penetrate the surface of the wood.

Oil   Oil is the easiest material to use and the most practical. Most oil finishes are relatively resistant to heat, water and alcohol, and are easy to maintain and repair. The finish improves with age, too. Never use oil inside a drawer or bookcase, however, or any place where cloth or paper will be stored. Most oil finishes will bleed or sweat on a hot day and cloth and paper will pick up the oil.

Linseed oil, which is made from the seed of the flax plant, is one of the oldest finishing materials, and for many years was the most commonly used. But even after lengthy drying, linseed oil never hardens through completely and, when used by itself, is not a durable finish. For many years I have used a three-step linseed-oil finish that is much more durable than plain linseed. Allow 24 hours of drying time between each coat.

For the first coat, mix half pure raw linseed oil and half pure turpentine. Put on a heavy coat with a rag and allow it to soak into the wood. (In between uses, I keep the rag in a closed container with the linseed oil.)

The next day apply the second coat, using pure boiled linseed oil. Leave it on for two to three hours, then sand the surface with some worn, fine sandpaper and wipe it clean.

On the third day apply the last coat. Mix half boiled linseed oil and half japan drier. When applying the finish, don't cover too large an area at one time. For example, if finishing a cabinet, first put the oil on one side, wait about ten minutes, and apply it to the other side. After ten minutes more, do the top. The reason for allowing the time between is that after a while the finish gets tacky — sometimes after twenty minutes and sometimes after five hours, depending on the drying conditions. When the finish gets tacky, you have to work fast, because it will dry suddenly. If you haven't allowed the ten minutes between areas, the finish on the last area will dry before you have a chance to wipe it off.

When the finish gets tacky, use a piece of burlap to rub the oil into the pores, going across the grain. Then wipe the extra oil off with a clean rag.

To prevent spontaneous combustion, put used burlap and rags in an airtight container or burn them.

On the fourth day, steelwool the surface and wipe it clean with a rag. For a shinier surface, sprinkle on some rottenstone and polish with a piece of leather, going with the grain. Rottenstone is one of the finest natural abrasives for polishing surfaces.

Linseed oil should not be used on eating utensils, but I used the finish just described on our kitchen counters and dining table 24 years ago, and the whole family is still healthy. There are salad-bowl finishes available, approved by the Food and Drug Administration, that are recommended for use on eating utensils.

The oil I use most now is Watco Danish Oil **(1)**, not because I am a Dane, but because it is easy to use and provides a durable finish. The way I use it is not the way recommended on the label, however. I put on a heavy first coat with a rag, but I don't wipe it off after 30 minutes — I leave it on.

1

The next day a lot of oil is left dried on the surface. I put on another coat of oil over this, which dissolves the surface residue. After five minutes, I sand with 220-grit paper **(2)**. This results in a thicker oil that helps to fill in the pores. The next day I steelwool with 3/0 steel wool, and the surface is finished.

Of all the different oil finishes, tung oil, which is extracted from the fruit of the tung tree, has the most resistance to water, acid, heat and mildew, but it takes a long time to dry. It is best to rub it into the wood with a small rag. After 24 hours a second coat can be applied. This results in a beautiful finish. All oils darken the wood to which they are applied, but tung oil darkens the wood the least. Linseed darkens wood the most, and Watco is in between tung and linseed.

Shellac Shellac, an organic material produced from the lac bug found in the Far East, is a good finishing material with several advantages. It's easy to use, is a durable, elastic finish that won't get air bubbles when applied, and dries fast. The disadvantage is that it is not water, heat and alcohol-proof. But it is easy to repair. If a shellac finish is exposed to a lot of sun for many years, it will, like any other finish, fade or change color. Applying thin oil, such as kerosene, to a shellac finish and leaving it on overnight won't damage the finish and will usually result in the return of the original color.

Shellac can be bought either as dry flakes or in liquid form. In liquid form it is sold as 2, 3 or 4-lb. cut, which refers to the amount of flakes dissolved in 1 gal. alcohol. Liquid shellac, especially white shellac, has a short shelf life. White shellac is simply flakes of orange shellac bleached and ground into granules. Even in dry form, white shellac has a shelf life of only three to six months, and I try to avoid using it.

Liquid shellac should have a date on the jar; don't use it after that date because it will never dry, and I mean *never* dry. I once made a cabinet with pull-out trays for canned goods and finished it with old shellac — after eight years, the shellac is still sticky. To get a tray out, you first have to hit it with your hand; then, to get the cans loose, you have to hit them, too. Of course, the advantage is that the cans never fall off the trays.

For best results, make your own shellac. Put some flakes of orange shellac in a jar, then pour denatured alcohol to cover them by 1 in. Immediately shake the jar for three to five minutes to prevent the flakes from gluing themselves together in a big lump. Shake every five minutes after that until all the flakes are dissolved.

Always keep liquid shellac in a glass or plastic jar. If kept in a metal container, the shellac will discolor and get a muddy look.

Shellac can be sprayed (p. 190), brushed or padded on. If you decide to spray, keep the pressure at about 25 lb. Pressure that is any higher will push out the shellac too quickly.

Most craftsmen prefer to apply shellac with a brush because it is not very difficult. Use a good brush that is made especially for applying varnish, enamel and shellac. It will cost a little more to buy but the end result will be well worth it. A 2-in. wide brush is good for all-around use.

If you use 2-lb. cut shellac, it will dry fast and won't leave brushmarks. It's best to brush it on in several thin coats rather than in one or two heavy ones. Apply the shellac going with the grain in long, full strokes. After covering the entire surface, wait five to ten minutes and then sand lightly with fine sandpaper — 220 grit is good. If more than two coats are applied, however, the shellac will take longer to dry.

2

Dry shellac will not stick to sandpaper, so if your shellac does, wait a little longer for it to dry. When sanding, be careful not to go through the finish. After sanding, wipe off the dust and apply another coat of shellac. Never use steel wool between coats: It breaks into small pieces that get stuck in the pores of the wood and make the finish rough. After the desired number of coats are applied, the surface can be rubbed out with 3/0 steel wool or scraped.

You can also pad on shellac for a smooth, shiny open-pored finish. (In French polishing, the traditional shellac finish, the pores are always filled.) Use the same type of pad described for use in French polishing (p. 196), but don't use the same pad for both finishes. This is because pumice and oil are used in French polishing, but not when applying a padded shellac finish.

For a padded shellac finish, first apply two coats of 2-lb. cut shellac with a brush. When the shellac is dry, sand the surface and wipe off the dust with a cloth. Now, put a little shellac into the pad — don't overdo it. Going with the grain, move the pad the full length of the piece, back and forth, over the surface. Continue until the pad is fairly dry. Then, if the surface does not look satisfactory, add a little more shellac to the pad and keep going. Never stop using the pad until it is fairly dry. If the finish is too shiny, wait until the surface is dry and lightly rub with 3/0 steel wool.

Any shellac finish can be removed easily with ammonia. Don't use alcohol because it is messy and will evaporate too fast. Also, ammonia is less expensive than alcohol.

The 4-F Finish An oil-and-shellac finish can be applied quickly and looks beautiful if done right. I first used this finish about 30 years ago, because of an accident. I had a shop with eight people working in it. One day, as we were loading a truck with furniture, one side of a cabinet got badly scratched. The furniture had a four-day oil finish and we didn't have time to redo it. As I was standing there, it occured to me that shellac and oil are used together for French polish, so I decided to take a chance. I scraped and sanded the damaged piece, put oil on and then shellac right over it. When the finish got tacky, I rubbed it out with steel wool and it came out as beautiful as the rest of the furniture. Since then, my students and I have frequently used this finish. When I first demonstrated it to them, the students named it the 4-F Finish: Frid's Fast Fine Finish.

For this finish I prefer to use raw linseed oil or Watco instead of boiled linseed oil, and orange shellac instead of white, because these make it easier to get a smooth finish. If a lot of pieces have to be finished, you could mix the oil and shellac together, but keep shaking the material as you use it. (I don't recommend doing this.)

Here's how to do the work. First put on a nice even coat of oil with a rag **(3)**. Immediately brush on a coat of 3-lb. cut shellac, using a cheap brush or a rag **(4)**. Keep testing the surface as it dries **(5)** until it is tacky. Don't let the surface get too dry or you will really have a problem getting all the shellac and oil off.

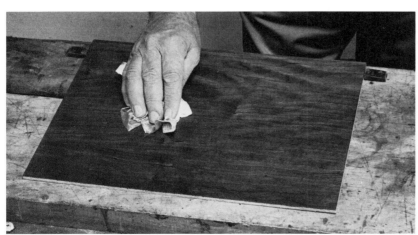

3

4

When the piece is tacky, rub it with a pad of 3/0 steel wool going with the grain **(6)** until all the shellac and oil are removed from the surface. If the pad gets saturated, use a new one. Be sure to remove all the oil and shellac from the surface and corners, or else the excess finish will turn gray.

Next wipe the surface clean with a dry cloth. You will have a finish that is as beautiful as a regular oil finish. If you want a higher shine, apply another coat of shellac immediately, but don't use any more oil. This picture **(7)** shows the finished piece.

This finish is best used on small pieces and on pieces that won't come in contact with water, such as chairs and table bases, because it is not waterproof and will spot if water is left on for a while. But this finish is easily repaired. Just put oil on the spot, steelwool or sand lightly and, after the spots disappear, wipe off all the excess oil.

If for some reason the piece gets dry and rough after it has been used for some time, put oil on and sand with 220-grit paper. Then wipe off all the excess oil immediately. If you don't, the finish will get tacky.

Never use an oil-and-shellac finish directly on top of a varnish or lacquer finish. For that matter, never put lacquer over an oil finish because the lacquer won't dry. If lacquer is used over varnish, the varnish will bubble up. If you feel you must put lacquer over an oil or varnish finish, you can use a sealer coat of shellac between the finishes because shellac will dry on any finish. But I don't like to do this.

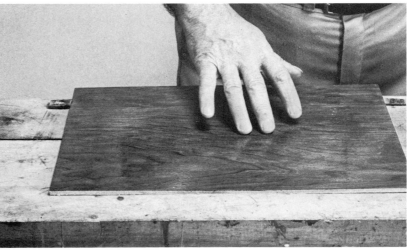

5

6

7

Lacquer When you want a glossy finish, use lacquer. Lacquer can be sprayed or brushed on and is considerably easier to use than French polish. It is also more resistant to water, alcohol and heat. A lacquer finish is very difficult to repair, but if the damage is simply water spots, these can be removed by moistening the finish with lacquer thinner using an atomizer or spray gun. Don't get the finish too wet — just keep it moist until the spots disappear. Never use lacquer on top of an oil or varnish finish because it will never dry.

Nitrate cellulose lacquer was introduced after World War I and is what most people use today instead of cellulose lacquer, which is made of cellulose dissolved in acetone. Cellulose lacquer will put on only a very thin film, which is fine for use on metal but I don't like to use it on wood. Each manufacturer has its own recipe for lacquer, so it is important to follow the directions for thinning that are given on the can you buy and to use the thinner that is recommended.

It is easier to spray on lacquer than it is to brush it on, but for spraying you need an air compressor, which is an expensive piece of equipment. A good compressor having two pistons will ensure constant pressure. You will also be able to use other pneumatic tools with a compressor, so get a good one. A cheap compressor used to spray a large surface might not be able to keep up the pressure and you'll wind up in big trouble. When you are spraying lacquer, keep the pressure at about 40 lb. to 50 lb.

The proportion of air to lacquer sprayed depends on the work you are doing. For small surfaces, use less air **(8)**; for large surfaces, more air **(9)**. The nozzle of a spray gun has three holes — lacquer is sprayed through the center hole and air through the hole on each side **(10)**. Air flow is regulated by twisting the knob shown **(11)**. This knob **(12)** controls the amount of lacquer. If your gun spits during spraying, check this hole **(13)**, which should be free of lacquer at all times. If the hole is clean and your gun still spits, you might be using lacquer that is too heavy.

Hold the gun about 6 in. to 8 in. away from the surface. Pressure and gun distance vary, depending on the work and the spraying equipment. Experience is the best teacher.

To spray, move the gun first across the grain **(14,15)**, then with the grain **(16)**, continuing the pattern to build up an even coat on the surface. The hardest thing to learn is when to stop spraying. Here's one way to tell. As the lacquer is forced out of the gun in small drops and hits the surface, the surface eventually begins to look like an orange peel. With the application of more lacquer, the orange-peel texture begins to disappear as all the small drops flow together. As soon as the orange-peel texture disappears, stop spraying or the lacquer will begin to run. This, of course, is if the piece is standing on end. If the piece is lying flat, you could apply more lacquer without danger of runs.

If you find some runs after the lacquer is completely dry, use a small mill file to smooth them before scraping. If the scraper were used before filing, it would pull off all the lacquer where the run is.

Many people spray on a coat of sanding sealer to seal the wood and fill the pores before applying lacquer. I never use sanding sealer because it makes you feel as if you are looking at the finished work through a film, and, after several years, there's a good chance that the sanding sealer will make the pores turn white. Depending on how open-pored the wood is, I usually just apply three coats of lacquer, scraping lightly in between coats. For a wood such as oak I'd probably use four coats.

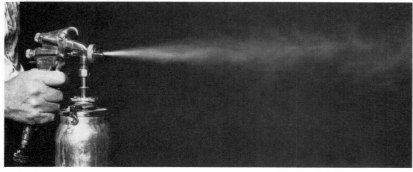

8

9

10

11

12

13

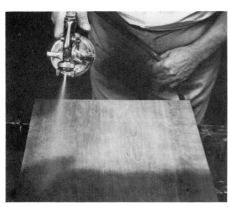

14

15

16

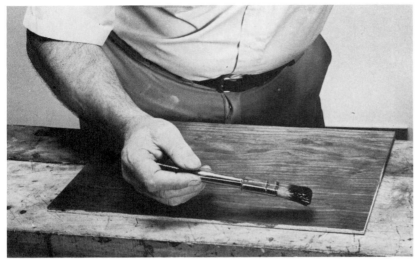

17

18

Using a brush to apply lacquer is very difficult. The first coat is easy, but because each new coat melts into the previous one, the second and third coats take more skill.

Always use a good-quality brush with soft hair to flow on the lacquer. Never brush it on like paint. Saturate the brush with lacquer, then bring it in like an airplane landing **(17,18)**. Move it all the way to the end of the work **(19)**.

19

Now reverse the stroke of the brush, moving it down on the surface in the same manner as before **(20)**. Never start the brush at the ends because lacquer will run down along the edges.

After completing the first track (which is the entire width of the brush), start the next one and continue in that way until the whole surface is covered. Never go back over the same track twice. If you do, it's possible that the brush might pick up three coats' worth of lacquer in some places and dump six coats' worth in others.

If the condition of the lacquer is right and it is applied correctly, it should flow out to a smooth finish. Lacquer that is too heavy will not flow out properly and air bubbles might become trapped, resulting in numerous pin holes in the finish. The biggest air bubbles can be removed while the finish is still soft. Puncture them carefully with a scriber **(21)** and the lacquer will flow back together.

Getting the lacquer mixture right takes practice and guesswork and depends on the type of lacquer you use. Once you decide on the type you prefer, you'll figure it out.

To estimate the drying time between coats of lacquer, whether sprayed or brushed, check the can to see what the manufacturer recommends. It's usually about four hours. The last coat should dry for 24 to 48 hours before being scraped and rubbed.

Never use steel wool between coats of lacquer because it breaks into small pieces that get stuck in the finish. And, because of the static electricity put into the steel from rubbing, the pieces will pull the lacquer up into many little pyramids. You could use a flat mill file to remove them, but it's better not to use steel wool in the first place.

Running a scraper blade lightly over the finish is an alternative to using steel wool and sandpaper between coats. Then wipe the finish with a clean rag and apply the next coat of lacquer. Make sure the scraper blade has a fine, smooth burr.

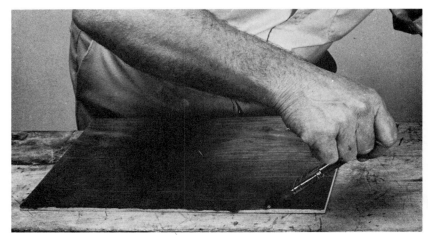

20

21

When I first came to the United States from Denmark to teach woodworking, the first question I was asked is how to finish lacquer. The students and the other teacher were spending a lot of time using wet sandpaper and rubbing the lacquer, but the result was unattractive — the finish still looked uneven, like an asphalt road after a shower. When I explained to them (using my arms and legs instead of English) that I scraped lacquer, they shook their heads and nobody wanted to talk to me. I soon realized that I was not really wanted there. After a couple of months I asked the other teacher if I was going to be sent back to Denmark and he said yes without a moment's hesitation.

After my contract I still had four months left before my departure, so I decided I might as well make some money before I had to leave. I asked if I could borrow a workbench and a set of tools. The next morning, the students helped me to get a plank of mahogany into the workshop before they went to design class (to which I was no longer invited). After four hours I had made a coffee table out of the mahogany. The base was sanded and the top screwed on, and I was sanding the top when the students returned. It was fun to see the looks on their faces when they saw the table ready to be finished; the table would have taken them more than a week to build because they did not know what they were doing. Anyway, I lacquered the table. When the lacquer dried, in front of the students, I scraped and buffed the tabletop in less than half an hour. After that day I never had a dull moment. So because of a coffee table and scraping lacquer, I was never forced to leave this country. Here is the table **(22)**, which my wife won't part with even after 32 years.

When scraping lacquer or shellac, start by going across the grain lightly on both ends first **(23)**, because the ends of a piece are the most difficult to get smooth. When they are smooth, continue scraping the whole surface, going with the grain.

Use the scraper blade in exactly the same way as explained in chapter 2 **(24,25)**. Keep crisscrossing the surface with the blade so that the finish will stay smooth and ungrooved. Before rubbing the finish, use the scraper the full length of the piece going with the grain to remove the marks on the ends made by scraping across the grain.

22

23

24

25

When using the scraper, be careful not to go through the finish. You will know that you have gone too far when you notice a change in color **(26)**. All finishes, including lacquer, darken the wood to some extent, so you know you've gone through when you see a lighter patch in the finish. If you do go through, use a half-dry brush to spot the finish with two or three coats of lacquer. Sand lightly between coats with 220-grit sandpaper, then give the whole surface a light coat of lacquer and scrape it again, which is easy because the surface is smooth and the pores are filled.

After the final scraping, rub with 3/0 steel wool if you want a dull finish. For a glossy finish, make a paste of 4F pumice and mineral oil and rub it on the surface with a felt block. You could also use a commercial rubbing compound. For a really high shine, follow up with rottenstone and oil, but wrap a clean cloth around the felt block to prevent scratches. To remove the oil, use either sanding dust or clean cloths.

There are other types of lacquer available that don't have to be rubbed, but these should be used only on cheap furniture. They are flat, semigloss and rub-effect lacquers. I never use them because they scratch too easily, and you don't get as nice a finish as when you scrape and rub a gloss lacquer. Plus, with these lacquers, you are really seeing the wood through a film, and a good finish should not hide the wood.

For objects such as small boxes, where you want to keep the wood light and just protect it from finger marks, one very thin coat of lacquer is a good finish. When it is dry, steel-wool it. The pores will be open and the surface will look as though it has an oil finish. But the lacquer finish is much lighter in color and will not bleed like an oil finish.

Varnish   I hardly ever use varnish, except for outdoor furniture or boat work. There are many different types of varnish available, and each is formulated for a special use. Some are resistant to water, alcohol, heat and scratches.

Varnish is much easier to apply than lacquer because the coats don't melt together, but because it takes so long to dry, dust is a problem. Varnish is also very difficult to repair and it looks like a film on top of the wood. The biggest problem with varnish is discoloration, especially if the varnished piece is exposed to a lot of light and sun.

Many modern synthetic finishes, such as polyurethane, state on the front of the can, in big letters, that they are guaranteed not to discolor for two years. But I certainly don't want to have to refinish my furniture every two years.   ☐

26

1

2

3

French Polishing

French polish is one of the most difficult finishes to learn to apply and one of the most time-consuming, but if a high-gloss finish is desired, I think a French-polished finish is the most beautiful one. French polishing brings out the beauty of the grain and gives the wood an almost three-dimensional feeling. A disadvantage of this finish is that it is not alcohol, water and heat-proof, but it is as easy to repair as shellac (p. 187).

Materials and equipment   First the pads — you will need at least two, one for polishing and one for clearing the finish of oil afterward. The pad for polishing should be proportionate in size to the area to be polished; for a surface of 3 sq. ft. to 4 sq. ft., the pad should be around 2 in. to 2½ in. in diameter. A smaller surface would call for a smaller pad and a larger surface for a larger pad. The pad for clearing should be about 1 in. in diameter. Any necessary patching or repair work will require a separate pad, which should also be about 1 in. in diameter.

Make each pad from a clean wool rag **(1)** packed into a hard ball. Wool is better than absorbent cotton, which is used when polishing moldings (p. 209), because wool mixes the shellac and alcohol and gives it up better than cotton.

Here is how to make a pad. First fold in all the corners of the rag toward the center **(2,3)**; keep stretching the wool.

When all the corners are pressed in, squeeze the pad into an oval while keeping the corners together in the center with your fingers **(4)**. The pad should be firm and hard **(5)**. Then wrap the pad tightly in a single thickness of colorless muslin or coarse linen **(6,7)**. This cloth is called the cover.

4

5

6

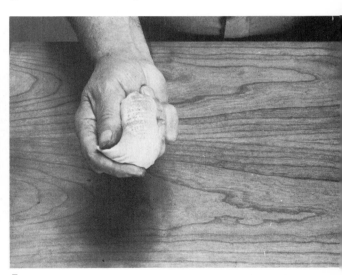

7

8

9

When not in use, keep the polishing pad in an airtight, covered container **(8,9)**. The pad will improve with age, becoming harder and keeping its shape better.

For French polishing, use only orange shellac of the highest quality. Orange shellac is even better if it is first filtered through a felt hat. The shellac will take days to go through the hat, but the result is a clear, burgundy-colored shellac with no impurities. It looks like wine, but don't drink it. This shellac will darken the wood very little. Never use white shellac on dark wood, as it will give the wood a gray color.

For solvent, use the highest grade of denatured alcohol you can find, not the ordinary commercial solvent sometimes sold for thinning shellac.

The use of boiled linseed oil as a lubricant, often recommended for French polishing, will cause the finish to sweat and eventually to turn slightly green. The best lubricant is paraffin or mineral oil.

Preparing the surface Carefully plane, scrape and sand the surface to be French polished. Remove or fill all imperfections, holes and marks. But don't fill the pores, because they will be filled during the first coat with pumice and shellac.

If the surface is to be stained, apply chemical or water stain before beginning to polish, then brush or spray on a sealer coat of 2-lb. cut shellac. This sealer coat is not absolutely necessary on unstained surfaces, but its application will make polishing easier. When thoroughly dry, sand the shellac lightly with 220-grit paper.

If the wood is the type that fuzzes up even after careful sanding, such as butternut, apply a coat of hot glue sizing (p. 135) to the surface and sand it smooth when dry to remove all excess. Don't use a shellac sealer coat if you're going to apply glue sizing. It's also a good idea to put a coat of sizing on veneer that shows any sign of checking.

The strokes   A French-polish finish should be stroked on with circular, oval or figure-eight motions. Circles should be approximately 4 in. to 6 in. in diameter, depending on the size of the pad; the strokes should completely cover the surface of the work. Never go over an area with the same stroke twice in a row because this will soften the finish, causing the pad to stick and roughen the area. (This is why it is more difficult to polish a small surface than a large one. On a small surface, the shellac doesn't have enough time to dry and settle into the pores between passes of the pad.)

Stroking too slowly, or stopping the pad for an instant while it is on the surface, may also roughen the finish, as will breaking circular strokes with an angular jag. It's a good idea for beginners to experiment with a dry pad before actually starting to work.

Because beginners tend to build up the center of a surface and neglect the edges and corners, concentrate first on learning how to stroke these areas. Be sure the pad overlaps the edges **(10)** when polishing there.

Corners are the most difficult. I've found that a good system is to hit the corner first at 45°, pushing the pad all the way off the surface **(11)**. The next time go across the grain, again pushing the pad off the surface **(12)**. Go with the grain next and, finally, go in circles.

Don't expect your first attempt at French polishing to produce a perfect finish. Experience and practice are better teachers than even the most detailed instructions.

10

11

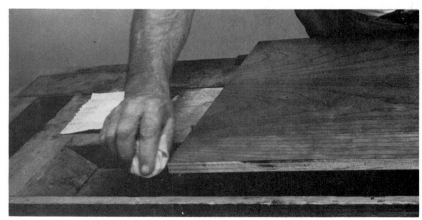

12

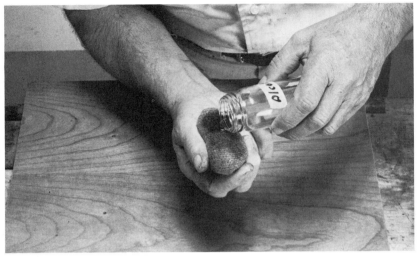

13

14

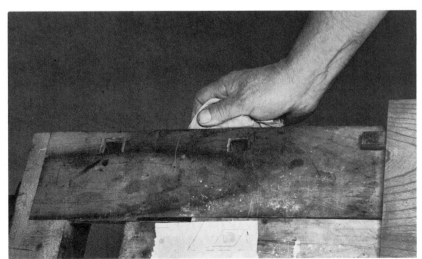

15

The first coat The first coat is the foundation of the entire French-polished finish, and great care must be taken to apply it evenly. During the first coat, the pores are filled with pumice and just enough shellac to bind the particles of pumice together.

If a sealer coat of shellac has been applied to the wood, very little shellac should be put into the wool of the pad at this stage. If you're using an old pad, there will probably be enough shellac left in it from the last time you used it. If you're using a new pad about 2½ in. in diameter, put about 1 tablespoon of shellac on the side of the wool that will be the bottom, then add about 2½ to 3 tablespoons of alcohol **(13)**. Put on the cloth cover and hit the pad against the side of your workbench **(14)** to mix the shellac and alcohol and make the polishing surface flat. Always do this whenever you add liquid to a pad. If it becomes too wet, squeeze out the excess liquid by clamping the pad firmly in a vise **(15)**.

If the wood has not been given a sealer coat of shellac, you'll need to put a little more shellac into the wool. About 2 tablespoons each of shellac and alcohol will do for a 2½-in. pad.

Alcohol softens a French-polished finish, and therefore too much pressure with an alcohol-saturated pad will result in an uneven surface. Shellac builds up the finish, but too much shellac will cause the pad to become sticky and prevent smooth polishing. In addition, too much shellac will cause the cover of the pad to become glazed with yellow or brown spots.

To begin polishing, first sprinkle some pumice lightly on the surface **(16)**. Put a small amount of pumice into a piece of linen and tie it into a ball **(17,18)**. This will allow you to shake fine pumice powder onto the wood. Too much pumice will build up in uneven patches and cause burns (p. 207). (If this happens, change the cover on your pad, which will pick up the extra pumice and eventually even out the burns.)

16

17

18

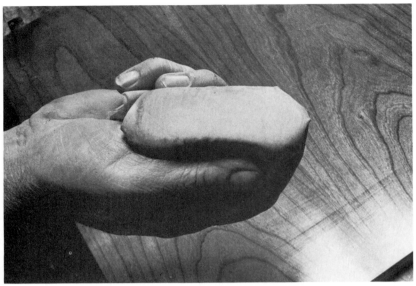

19

20

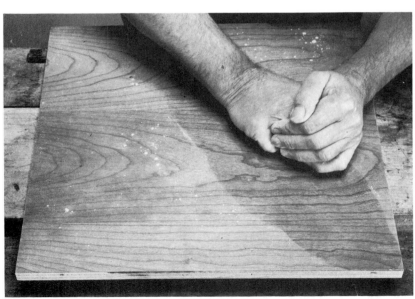

21

Begin to stroke on the polish, keeping the pad cover tightly over the wool for a firm, smooth polishing surface. Hold the pad in your fist so that pressure is directly under your knuckles **(19)**, not under the extended fingers. In the application of all coats of French polish, only light pressure is required when the pad is wet and the coat is being built up, so use only one hand **(20)**. As the pad dries out, there should be some pull against the surface but not enough to prevent steady strokes. Heavier pressure is required as the pad dries, because then the pad's function changes from building up to smoothing out. Use both hands **(21)**, but increase the pressure gradually — too much pressure when the pad is not dry enough may cause large swirls to stand out, leaving marks on the finish. If continued, this could even cause the finish to burn. Remember never to allow the pad to touch the surface being polished unless the pad is in motion. An instant's hesitation while the pad is in contact with the work might leave an unsightly blemish. Experience will tell you when to add more shellac, alcohol or pumice to the work.

Sometimes a piece of dust gets stuck in the finish **(22)**. Remove it with a sharp chisel while the finish is still soft **(23)** and continue.

The proper temperature for French polishing is 70°F or higher, so if the surface becomes cloudy while you are polishing, the room in which you are working is probably too cold. Never store the work in a cold room.

When all the pores are filled with pumice and shellac, and the pad is half dry, sprinkle on some paraffin oil and continue polishing with the same motions. Paraffin oil is necessary to build up a smooth finish and to help prevent burns, though sometimes, with open-pored wood such as oak, it is better not to use oil in the first coat. When starting the second coat on open-pored wood, don't use oil until the pores are completely refilled.

To apply the oil, dip a fingertip in and shake it here and there over the work **(24,25)**. One sprinkle at a time is enough. Too much oil will cause the pad to ride on an oily surface and lose contact with the work. Too little oil will cause burns.

22

23

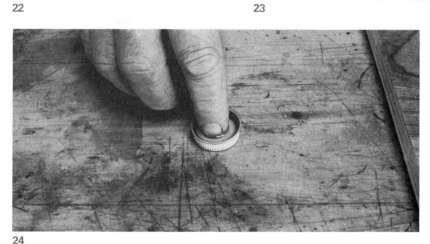

24

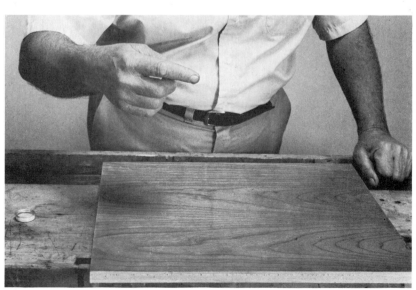

25

After you start to use oil on the surface, you should no longer apply pumice directly to the work. Sprinkle it lightly on the wool of the pad instead (26).

Apply both shellac and alcohol to the top of the wool, as necessary, so they can work out slowly to the bottom of the pad. Sprinkle on more oil if none shows on the surface when you test it occasionally by wiping it with your finger. An excess of alcohol in the pad will cause the oil to disappear from the surface too quickly.

Application of the first coat is completed when the surface is entirely covered with shellac and is free of swirls and blemishes, and when the pad is half dry. This usually takes about one hour. The application of a coat of French polish — any coat — is not complete until the pad becomes half dry, so when the pad just begins to dry, do not stop polishing. If you put aside the pad to rest or have a smoke, evaporation will dry the pad out in the air instead of on the work surface. So don't rest or smoke.

If, after application of this or any other coat, the surface is rough or uneven, allow it to dry at least one day, then rub it smooth with a felt block, pumice and paraffin oil before applying the next coat. For this you may also use 220-grit sandpaper and paraffin oil. But never use sandpaper, pumice and oil just before the final coat, because scratches will show up.

The second coat   After the first coat has been allowed to dry for at least one day, you are ready to apply the second coat. During the second coat you must fill the pores again, because the drying of the finish causes the pores to reappear slightly. After filling them, the idea is to get the surface built up with a thin layer of shellac as quickly as possible. Remember, when the pad is wet it puts on shellac, but as the pad dries out it is primarily smoothing the surface, although it continues to put on a little shellac.

Using the same pad you used for the first coat, add first a little shellac and then a little alcohol to the top of the wool. Sprinkle a little pumice between the wool and the cover. Pumice between wool and cover is necessary during the entire second coat.

Also sprinkle the surface of the work with a few drops of paraffin oil, if oil has been used in the first coat. Keep a little oil on the surface at all times — not so much that the pad will lose contact with the work, but not so little that the surface will scratch.

26

Stroke the pad with firm pressure, using the same motions as before. When the pad is working properly, you'll feel a very slight pull as you move it over the surface of the work and hear a slight rasping noise as the pumice works through the cover. The path left by the pad should be slightly dull, in contrast to the shinier surface that is on each side of the path. If this is not the case, try adding in turn shellac or alcohol until the path looks and feels right.

Keep an eye on the cover of the pad. If it wears out **(27)**, the pumice will come out too fast and damage the surface. If the pad cover turns yellow or becomes too sticky for smooth rubbing, add alcohol to the wool from the top and hit the pad firmly against the bench. Then continue rubbing, adding shellac, alcohol and pumice until the surface is smooth.

This coat, too, is completed when the pad is half dry and when the final strokes of the pad leave no marks on the surface. The finish should be clear and glossy and there should be no imperfections or blemishes. For the beginner, the application of the second coat will take about an hour. If possible, the second coat should be allowed to dry for at least two days.

The final coat   The third coat is usually the final coat. For this coat it's necessary to add a little 2-lb. cut shellac and alcohol to the wool of the pad. If small ridges and depressions appear in the surface as you polish, add a little more alcohol and stroke the surface lightly with the grain. Never use a pad that is too wet for this coat, because it will cause burns and you'll wind up having to apply another coat. Keep a light dusting of pumice between the wool and the cover, and sprinkle paraffin oil on the surface as you work. Work with varying strokes as when applying previous coats. Remember to keep the pad under your fists.

When the coat is built up to your satisfaction, touch the surface with your fingertip and move it lightly across the work to see whether the pad is leaving any marks. This cuts across the streaks. When the process is ended, the surface should have no marks.

To speed up this coat you can sprinkle on oil more frequently than before, after the pad is half dry, but still apply only a little at a time. Using more oil in the final coat than in the previous coats will help prevent scratches.

When the final coat is done, immediately clear the finish.

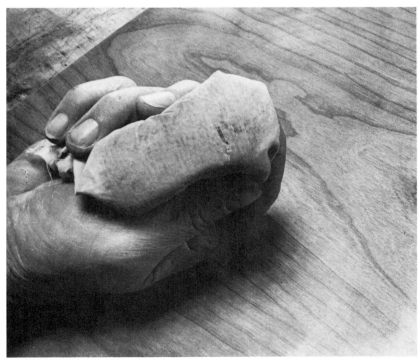

28

29

Clearing The clearing operation removes the oil film from the finish. You will need a fresh pad for this, one that has not been used for polishing. The pad should be about one third the size of the polishing pad and made out of the same material. You may use the clearing pad several times, but there is a limit to its life span. Never use a clearing pad for anything else, and store it in an airtight container when not in use.

To begin, moisten a clean clearing pad with alcohol, but don't get it too wet. Put a clean cloth over the wool and rub the work with long strokes going with the grain. As the pad dries, apply a little more pressure. During this operation, keep moving the cover of the pad over as it becomes saturated with oil, so you present a fresh surface to the work. Continue to move the pad up and down with the grain, running off the edge each time. This operation should remove all oil from the surface and leave a clear, bright finish. Clearing is completed when all oil is removed.

Experienced French-polishers often spit on the finish during clearing to speed it up. If you do this, I advise you not to have a dry martini right before you spit.

Dull finish If a dull finish is desired, two coats of French polish are usually sufficient, and the clearing operation is not required. Keep a light dusting of pumice between the wool and the cover, and sprinkle paraffin oil on the surface as you work. The second coat should be completed when the pad is quite dry. To dull the finish, sprinkle it with pumice and rub thoroughly with a clean shoe brush, always following the direction of the grain **(28,29)**. The pumice will pick up the oil. For a less dull finish, allow the work to dry at least 24 hours before brushing with pumice. □

Burning

The most common defect to appear in a surface being French polished is called burning. This is the buildup of dull, rough spots caused by adhesion of too much pumice to the tacky surface. Burn spots may vary in size from small dots to blemishes that cover the entire surface **(1,2)**. If burning occurs before paraffin oil has been applied to the work (early in the first coat), smooth out the area by rubbing vigorously with a pad moistened in alcohol. When attempting to erase a burn this way, move the cover of the pad frequently so that a fresh surface is always presented to the work to pick up the extra pumice.

If a burn is very heavy, use a sharp chisel to peel off its outer surface **(3)** before using the moist pad to smooth it out completely. But never use a chisel to remove burns in the final coat or after oil has been used. When the burn has been smoothed out, stroke that area more often than the rest of the surface to build up the removed polish.

If oil has been used on the work, apply a little more oil and rub the whole surface with circular and figure-eight strokes, concentrating on the burn until it disappears. If a burn is not removed by this method, leave the work until the next day, then sand the burn off with 220-grit sandpaper lubricated with paraffin oil. Proceed to build up the surface around the burn in the usual manner.   □

1

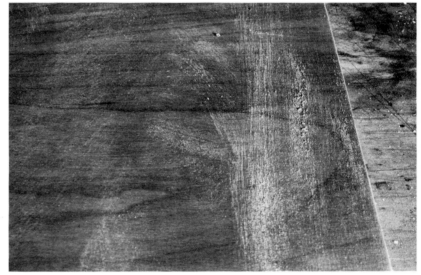

2

3

Repairing French Polish

If at any time in the French-polishing process you discover small holes or pits in the surface, perhaps spots you didn't notice in final sanding or filling, you should level them immediately with the following technique.

Pour ½ pint of 4-lb. or 5-lb. cut shellac into a clean tin can. Ignite the surface of the shellac and allow the alcohol to burn off until the volume of the liquid remaining is approximately half the original. Extinguish the flame by covering the can. Be careful.

To the remaining heavy shellac, stir in 1⅖ oz. (40 grams) of 4F pumice and 4 teaspoons of paraffin oil. Let the mixture cool. It should be the consistency of thick molasses. You may store it for future use, but if the mixture becomes too thick, add shellac to bring it back to the proper consistency.

Now, get your polishing pad working properly, as in the final coat. Then sharpen a piece of ¼-in. dowel to a pencil point. Dip the point in the mixture and place the drop that clings to its end in the hole to be filled. Take your polishing pad and hammer it down sharply over the drop; at the same instant the pad touches the work, glide off into a French-polishing stroke. Don't let the pad linger, but immediately stroke it over the surface. If you don't quite fill the hole, repeat the process, but do not repeat more than twice without polishing over the entire surface several times.

To erase small dents that have not broken the fibers of the wood on old French-polished finishes, first cover the dent with paraffin oil. Then place a piece of moist paper over the oil to moisten the surface and help raise the dent. Drop hot stick shellac on the paper directly over the dent. Melt the shellac drop from its stick with either a burning-in knife or a match. Repeat, if necessary, until the surface is flush.

To repair large indentations or bruises that are not too deep on old French-polished finishes, again pour paraffin oil over the damaged area. Prepare a small torch by wrapping a piece of cotton around the end of a wire and wetting the cotton with alcohol. Ignite the torch and pass it quickly over the surface of the oil, but be careful not to get the oil so hot that it bubbles up on the surface, because you might burn the finish. If the dents are not filled all the way, level them off with the heavy shellac mixture.

To build up repaired areas or to refinish spots, make up a small pad about the size of a fifty-cent piece, depending on the size of the damage, of course. Use the same material as for a polishing pad. If you are using the pad for the first time, moisten the wool with 2-lb. cut shellac; if you've used the pad before, moisten the wool with alcohol. Dust pumice over the wool before covering it, and follow the regular French-polishing technique, at first confining your strokes to as small an area as possible around the repair. Finish up by widening your circles around the repaired area to blend it into the surrounding area. It's a good idea to French polish a small scrap of wood when the surface being repaired is drying, to keep the pad working. Don't forget to clear the finish of oil, as described on p. 206. If you like, dull the spot with pumice and a shoe brush. ☐

French Polishing Moldings

Moldings should always be French polished before beginning the main surface. To do this, use a pad of absorbent cotton without any cover. Pour some 2-lb. cut shellac, alcohol and paraffin oil directly onto the cotton **(1)** and dust pumice over it **(2)**. Squeeze the pad to mix the shellac, alcohol and oil and to remove excess liquid **(3)**.

Now rub the molding with continuous strokes **(4)**. Because of the size of molding, it's possible to use only straight back-and-forth strokes. (The oil prevents the shellac from turning into a sticky mess, so this is why oil is used in the first coat.) As you proceed, the pad will shape itself to the contour of the molding.

1

2

3

4

Slight alterations to this shape may occur when you add shellac or pumice to the pad, but try to maintain the contour as closely as possible to prevent streaking. Apply as many coats of French polish to the molding as you intend to apply to the main body of the work, using the technique just described for each one. Allow drying time of at least two days between coats.

The clearing operation for molding is quite different from that used on the main surface of the work. First, rub the molding with a dry, clean rag to remove as much oil as possible. Next, soak a piece of absorbent cotton with 4-lb. or 5-lb. cut shellac **(5)**. Move the wet cotton along the molding with a single stroke. When dry, the molding is finished. □

French Polishing Turnings

To French polish work on the lathe, use the same type of pad and material used for French polishing moldings. Run the lathe at very low speed and apply the polish along the moving surface of the work. Clearing may be done by either of two methods: For a large piece, use alcohol as described on p. 206 or, for small, intricate turnings, use heavy shellac as described in the clearing operation for moldings.

I like to use Qualasole, a padding lacquer especially formulated for use on turnings, as a modern-day French polish. □

5